Dedication & Acknowledgments

This book is dedicated to the students and teachers who have used *ACTIVE Skills for Reading* over the past ten years. Since 2002/2003 when the first edition of *ACTIVE Skills for Reading* was published, thousands of students and teachers have used the book. I know that I had no idea that the series would be this popular and that we would reach the stage of publishing a third edition.

The pedagogical framework for this series is as viable today as it has ever been. As students and teachers use each of the elements of *ACTIVE*, stronger reading will result.

My associations with the editorial team in Singapore continue to be some of my greatest professional relationships. I express appreciation to Sean Bermingham, Derek Mackrell, Andrew Robinson, and Sarah Tan for their commitment to excellence in publishing. I also express appreciation to Jenny Wilsen and John Murn for their commitment to helping the third edition be stronger than the two previous editions.

Neil J Anderson

The third edition of *ACTIVE Skills for Reading* maintains the *ACTIVE* approach developed by reading specialist Professor Neil J Anderson, while introducing several significant improvements.

This new edition now has a full color design, presenting the series' content in an attractive and student-friendly way. Approximately half of the passages have been replaced with new and engaging topics; the rest have been updated. It also has a wide variety of text types including articles, journals, blogs, and interviews, with later levels featuring readings based on content from National Geographic.

Each of the 24 chapters now includes a "Motivational Tips" section from Professor Anderson, reflecting his current research into student motivation and learning. His reading charts have also been updated to more accurately track students' reading fluency and comprehension progress.

ACTIVE Skills for Reading, Third Edition features an Assessment CD-ROM with ExamView® Pro, which has been revised to reflect the needs of learners preparing for standardized tests.

This latest edition of Active Skills for Reading series is designed to further enhance students' progress, helping them to become more confident, independent, and active readers.

Reviewers for this edition

Mardelle Azimi; **Jose Carmona** Hillsborough Community College; **Grace Chao** Soochow University; **Mei-Rong Alice Chen** National Taiwan University of Science and Technology; **Irene Dryden; Jennifer Farnell** Greenwich Japanese School; **Kathy Flynn** Glendale Community College; **Sandy Hartmann** University of Houston; **Joselle L. LaGuerre; Margaret V. Layton; Myra M. Medina** Miami Dade College; **Masumi Narita** Tokyo International University; **Margaret Shippey** Miami Dade College; **Satoshi Shiraki; Karen Shock** Savannah College of Art and Design; **Sandrine Ting; Colin S. Ward** Lonestar College; **Virginia West** Texas A&M University; **James B. Wilson; Ming-Nuan Yang** Chang Gung Institute of Technology; **Jakchai Yimngam** Rajamangala University of Technology

Reviewers of the second edition

Chiou-lan Chern National Taiwan Normal University; **Cheongsook Chin** English Campus Institute, Inje University; **Yang Hyun** Jung-Ang Girls' High School; **Li Junhe** Beijing No.4 High School; **Tim Knight** Gakushuin Women's College; **Ahmed M. Motala** University of Sharjah; **Gleides Ander Nonato** Colégio Arnaldo and Centro Universitário Newton Paiva; **Ethel Ogane** Tamagawa University; **Seung Ku Park** Sunmoon University; **Shu-chien, Sophia, Pan** College of Liberal Education, Shu-Te University; **Marlene Tavares de Allmeida** Wordshop Escola de Linguas; **Naowarat Tongkam** Silpakorn University; **Nobuo Tsuda** Konan University; **Hasan Hüseyin Zeyrek** Istanbul Kültür University Faculty of Economics and Administrative Sciences

Contents

THIRD EDITION

ACTIVE

SKILLS FOR READING STUDENT BOOK 1

Neil J Anderson

NATIONAL GEOGRAPHIC LEARNING

HEINLE
CENGAGE Learning

Australia • Brazil • Japan • Korea • Mexico • Singapore • Spain • United Kingdom • United States

Active Skills for Reading Student Book 1, Third Edition
Neil J Anderson

Publisher, Asia and Global ELT:
Andrew Robinson

Senior Development Editor: Derek Mackrell

Associate Development Editor: Sarah Tan, Claire Tan

Director of Global Marketing: Ian Martin

Academic Marketing Manager: Emily Stewart

Marketing Communications Manager:
Beth Leonard

Director of Content and Media Production:
Michael Burggren

Associate Content Project Manager:
Mark Rzeszutek

Manufacturing Manager: Marcia Locke

Manufacturing Planner:
Mary Beth Hennebury

Composition: PreMediaGlobal

Cover Design: Page2, LLC

For product information and technology assistance, contact us at
Cengage Learning Customer & Sales Support, 1-800-354-9706

For permission to use material from this text or product, submit all requests online at **cengage.com/permissions**
Further permissions questions can be emailed to
permissionrequest@cengage.com

ISBN-13: 978-1-133-30799-0
ISBN-10: 1-133-30799-X

National Geographic Learning
20 Channel Center Street
Boston, MA 02210
USA

Cengage Learning is a leading provider of customized learning solutions with office locations around the globe, including Singapore, the United Kingdom, Australia, Mexico, Brazil, and Japan. Locate your local office at:
international.cengage.com/region

Cengage Learning products are represented in Canada by Nelson Education, Ltd.

Visit Heinle online at **elt.heinle.com**

Visit our corporate website at **www.cengage.com**

Photo credits
FRONT MATTER: Thinkstock: Hemera/Getty Images, Jupiterimages/Getty Images, Jupiterimages/Getty Images, Hemera/Getty Images. **p11:** Thinkstock (all). **p13:** Featureflash/Shutterstock (tr), Courtesy of David Loftus (cr). **p16:** Hemera/Thinkstock (tl, tr), iStockphoto/Thinkstock (cl, cr). **p17:** Marie C Fields/Shutterstock. **p21:** iStockphoto/Thinkstock (tl, tr, bl), Moreno Soppelsa/Shutterstock (tc), Stockbyte/Thinkstock (bc), Photodisc/Thinkstock (br). **p23:** Ben Hider/Getty Images. **p27:** iStockphoto/Thinkstock (tl, bl), James Woodson/Digital Vision/Thinkstock (cl). **p30:** iStockphoto/Thinkstock. **p31:** Hemera/Thinkstock(l, tr), iStockphoto/Thinkstock (cr). **p33:** violetkaipa/Shutterstock. **p37:** Jenkedco/Shutterstock (tr), Jupiterimages/Comstock/Thinkstock (tl). **p41:** Carlos E. Santa Maria/Shutterstock. **p42:** Blend_Images/iStockphoto. **p45:** Copyright T. VanCleave, totallyabsurd (all). **p47:** Maxim Petrichuk/Shutterstock (tr), Iakov Filimonov/Shutterstock (cl), Darren Baker/Shutterstock (bl). **p49:** Dusan Jankovic/Shutterstock (bl), Creatas/Thinkstock (tc), Stockbyte/Thinkstock (tr), iStockphoto/Thinkstock (bc), Comstock/Thinkstock (br), Thinkstock (cl). **p51:** Getty Images/Comstock/Thinkstock (tr), Brand X Pictures/Thinkstock (cr). **p55:** Creatas Images/Thinkstock. **p59:** Vladimir Mucibabic/Shutterstock (tl). **p60:** Goodshot/Thinkstock (tl), Keith Brofsky/Stockbyte/Thinkstock (tc), Steve Mason/Photodisc/Thinkstock (br), Hemera/Thinkstock (tr), Fuse/Thinkstock (bl), Hemera Technologies/AbleStock/Thinkstock (bc). **p61:** Stockbyte/Thinkstock (tl), CREATISTA/Shutterstock (r). **p65:** Courtesy of TripIt (cr), Courtesy of WCities (br). **pg 69:** Sportsphotographer.eu,2010/Shutterstock (tl), sportgraphic/Shutterstock (tr), Diego Barbieri/Shutterstock (bl), Pete Niesen/Shutterstock (br). **p71:** Sergei Bachlakov/Shutterstock (t), The Asahi Shimbun/Getty Images (cr), SIMON TREW/AFP/Getty Images (bl). **p75:** corepics/Shutterstock (tl), EITAN ABRAMOVICH/AFP/Getty Images (cl), IPK Photography/Shutterstock (bl). **p80:** shock/Shutterstock (cl), Duck Brands(br). **p83:** Petro Feketa/iStockphoto (cl), Monkey Business Images/Shutterstock (cr). **p85:** Sergei Bachlakov,2010/Shutterstock (tr), ANNE-CHRISTINE POUJOULAT/AFP/Getty Images (cl), AP Photo/Jay LaPrete (br). **pg 87:** JingAiping/Shutterstock (tl), SeanPavonePhoto/Shutterstock (tr), Korea Tourism Organization (cl), Perov Stanislav/Shutterstock (cr). **p88:** iStockphoto/Thinkstock (tl, tc), Natalia Bratslavsky/Shutterstock (tr). **p89:** nimu1956/iStockphoto (r), Dinodia Photo/Age Fotostock (tl), LH Images/Alamy (bl). **p92:** anderm/Shutterstock (tl), PHB.cz (Richard Semik)/Shutterstock (tr), PRILL Mediendesign und Fotografie/Shutterstock (cl), AP Photo/Graziano Arici/New Venice Consortium, h.o. (cr). **p93:** CraigBurrows/Shutterstock (tl), wwwebmeister/Shutterstock (l, r). **p99:** Christopher Ewing/Shutterstock (tl), Thinkstockphoto (br). **pg 102:** Ryan Carter/Shutterstock. **p103:** AP Photo/Mark Gilliland (br). **p107:** © Getty Images (tl), jbor/Shutterstock (tr), JeremyRichards/Shutterstock (bl), gary718/Shutterstock (br). **p109:** Sawayasu Tsuji/iStockphoto (tr), gary yim/Shutterstock (br). **p113:** Stephen Finn/Shutterstock (tr, cl), Thinkstockphoto (br). **p115:** fredredhat/Shutterstock (all). **pg118:** Sandra Teddy/Getty Images (tr), Beano5/iStockphoto (cl), FaceMePLS/Flickr (br). **p121:** David P. Smith/Shutterstock. **p123:** Jarrod Hall /Demotix/Demotix/Corbis. **p125:** Andresr/Shutterstock (tl), Thinkstock (tc), Stephen Coburn/Shutterstock (bc), Hemera/Thinkstockphoto (tr), Thinkstockphoto (bl), Alexander Raths/Shutterstock (br). **p127:** Wavebreak Media/Thinkstockphoto (tr), Brand X Pictures/Thinkstockphoto (l), wdeon/Shutterstock (br). **p131:** Jason Stitt/Shutterstock (tr), fotoluminate/Shutterstock (cr), WizData, inc./Shutterstock (br). **p.135:** kwest/Shutterstock (tl), newphotoservice/Shutterstock (cl), 1971yes/Shutterstock (tr), Carlo Taccari/Shutterstock (cr). **p136:** Viktoria/Shutterstock. **p137:** Sergey Mikhaylov/Shutterstock (tr), alison1414/Shutterstock (tr), Cory Thoman/Shutterstock (l). **p145:** World History Archive/Alamy (l), Robert Browning/Getty Images (c), SuperStock/Getty Images (r). **pg147:** mario babu/Shutterstock (background), graph/shutterstock (r). **pg151:** Andre Maritz/Shutterstock. **pg156:** Dmitriy Shironosov/Shutterstock. **pg159:** Emilie Duchesne/istockphoto. **pg161:** maxuser/iStockphoto (tr), AP Photo (bl).

Printed in China
8 9 10 11 22 21 20 19

Vocabulary Learning Tips

Learning new vocabulary is an important part of learning to be a good reader. Remember that the letter **C** in **ACTIVE Skills for Reading** reminds us to **cultivate** vocabulary.

1 *Decide if the word is worth learning now*

As you read, you will find many words you do not know. You will slow your reading fluency if you stop at every new word. For example, you should stop to find out the meaning of a new word if:

a. you read the same word many times.

b. the word appears in the heading of a passage, or in the topic sentence of a paragraph—the sentence that gives the main idea of the paragraph.

2 *Record information about new words you decide to learn*

Keep a vocabulary notebook in which you write words you want to remember. Complete the following information for words that you think are important to learn:

New word	healthy
Translation	健康
Part of speech	adjective
Sentence where found	Oliver is well-known for sharing his secrets of cooking healthy food.
My own sentence	I exercise to stay fit and healthy.

3 *Learn words from the same family*

For many important words in English that you will want to learn, the word is part of a word family. As you learn new words, learn words in the family from other parts of speech (nouns, verbs, adjectives, adverbs, etc.).

Noun	happiness
Verb	
Adjective	happy
Adverb	happily

4 *Learn words that go with the key word you are learning*

When we learn new words, it is important to learn what other words are frequently used with them. These are called collocations. Here is an example from a student's notebook.

		long		
take		two-week		next week
go on	a	short	vacation	in Italy
need		summer		with my family
have		school		by myself

5 *Create a word web*

A word web is a picture that helps you connect words together and helps you increase your vocabulary. Here is a word web for the word *frightened*:

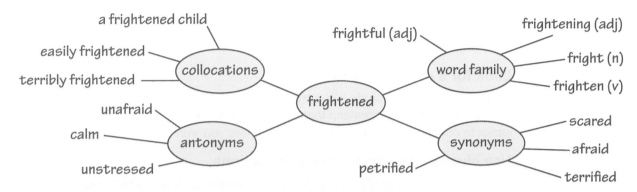

6 *Memorize common prefixes, roots, and suffixes*

Many English words can be divided into different parts. We call these parts *prefixes*, *roots*, and *suffixes*. A *prefix* comes at the beginning of a word, a *suffix* comes at the end of a word, and the *root* is the main part of the word. In your vocabulary notebook, make a list of prefixes and suffixes as you come across them. On page 175 there is a list of prefixes and suffixes in this book. For example, look at the word *unhappily*.

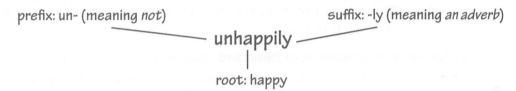

prefix: un- (meaning *not*) suffix: -ly (meaning *an adverb*)

unhappily

root: happy

7 *Regularly review your vocabulary notebook*

You should review the words in your vocabulary notebook very often. The more often you review your list of new words, the sooner you will be able to recognize the words when you see them during reading. Set up a schedule to go over the words you are learning.

8 *Make vocabulary flash cards*

Flash cards are easy to make, and you can carry them everywhere with you. You can use them to study while you are waiting for the bus, walking to school or work, or eating a meal. You can use the flash cards with your friends to quiz each other. Here is an example of a flash card:

translation

potong

cut

example sentence

He is cutting an apple.

Front   Back

Tips for Fluent Reading

Find time to read every day.

Find the best time of day for you to read. Try to read when you are not tired. By reading every day, even for a short period, you will become a more fluent reader.

Look for a good place to read.

It is easier to read and study if you are comfortable. Make sure that there is good lighting in your reading area and that you are sitting in a comfortable chair. To make it easier to concentrate, try to read in a place where you won't be interrupted.

Use clues in the text to make predictions.

Fluent readers make predictions before and as they read. Use the title, subtitle, pictures, and captions to ask yourself questions about what you are going to read. Find answers to the questions when you read. After reading, think about what you have learned and decide what you need to read next to continue learning.

Establish goals before you read.

Before you read a text, think about the purpose of your reading. For example, do you just want to get a general idea of the passage? Or do you need to find specific information? Thinking about what you want to get from the reading will help you decide what reading skills you need to use.

Notice how your eyes and head are moving.

Good readers use their eyes, and not their heads, when they read. Moving your head back and forth when reading will make you tired. Practice avoiding head movements by placing your elbows on the table and resting your head in your hands. Do you feel movement as you read? If you do, hold your head still as you read. Also, try not to move your eyes back over a text. You should reread part of a text only when you have a specific purpose for rereading, for example, to make a connection between what you read previously and what you are reading now.

Try not to translate.

Translation slows down your reading. Instead of translating new words into your first language, first try to guess the meaning. Use the context (the other words around the new word) and word parts (prefixes, suffixes, and word roots) to help you guess the meaning.

Read in phrases rather than word by word.

Don't point at each word while you read. Practice reading in phrases—groups of words that go together.

Engage your imagination.

Good readers visualize what they are reading. They create a movie in their head of the story they are reading. As you read, try sharing with a partner the kinds of pictures that you create in your mind.

Avoid subvocalization.

Subvocalization means quietly saying the words as you read. You might be whispering the words or just silently saying them in your mind. Your eyes and brain can read much faster than you can speak. If you subvocalize, you can only read as fast as you can say the words. As you read, place your finger on your lips or your throat. Do you feel movement? If so, you are subvocalizing. Practice reading without moving your lips.

Don't worry about understanding every word.

Sometimes, as readers, we think we must understand the meaning of everything that we read. It isn't always necessary to understand every word in a passage in order to understand the meaning of the passage as a whole. Instead of interrupting your reading to find the meaning of a new word, circle the word and come back to it after you have finished reading.

Enjoy your reading.

Your enjoyment of reading will develop over time. Perhaps today you do not like to read in English, but as you read more, you should see a change in your attitude. The more you read in English, the easier it will become. You will find yourself looking forward to reading.

Read as much as you can.

The best tip to follow to become a more fluent reader is to read whenever and wherever you can. Good readers read a lot. They read many different kinds of material: newspapers, magazines, textbooks, websites, and graded readers. To practice this, keep a reading journal. Every day, make a list of the kinds of things you read during the day and how long you read each for. If you want to become a more fluent reader, read more!

Are You an ACTIVE Reader?

Before you use this book to develop your reading skills, think about your reading habits, and your strengths and weaknesses when reading in English. Check the statements that are true for you.

		Start of course	End of course
1	I read something in English every day.	☐	☐
2	I try to read where I'm comfortable and won't be interrupted.	☐	☐
3	I make predictions about what I'm going to read before I start reading.	☐	☐
4	I think about my purpose of reading before I start reading.	☐	☐
5	I keep my head still, and move only my eyes, when I read.	☐	☐
6	I try not to translate words from English to my first language.	☐	☐
7	I read in phrases rather than word by word.	☐	☐
8	I try to picture in my mind what I'm reading.	☐	☐
9	I read silently, without moving my lips.	☐	☐
10	I try to understand the meaning of the passage, and try not to worry about understanding the meaning of every word.	☐	☐
11	I usually enjoy reading in English.	☐	☐
12	I try to read as much as I can, especially outside class.	☐	☐

Follow the tips on pages 8–9. These will help you become a more active reader. At the end of the course, answer this quiz again to see if you have become a more fluent, active reader.

Getting Ready

Discuss the following questions with a partner.
1 What foods do you see in the pictures?
2 Which ones do you like? Which ones don't you like?
3 Do you like to cook? What dishes can you cook?

CHAPTER 1 A Restaurant for Change

Before You Read
Learning to Cook

A **Think about answers to the following questions.**

    1 What are some ways people learn how to cook?

    _____   _____

    _____   _____

    2 Which of these ways would be useful for someone learning how to cook as a job?

B **Discuss your answers with a partner.**

Reading Skill
Predicting

> Before reading, good readers think about what they are going to read. And while reading, they think about what comes next. This helps them better understand what they are reading.

A **Look at the pictures and title of the passage on the next page. Then answer this question.**

How can a restaurant change a person's life?

B **Read paragraphs 1 and 2 in the passage. Then answer the following questions.**

    1 Were your predictions in A correct?
    2 What kind of training do you think the young chefs at Fifteen get?

C **Read paragraph 3 in the passage. Then answer the following questions.**

    1 Were your predictions in B correct?
    2 Why do you think the restaurant is named Fifteen?

D **Read the last paragraph in the passage. Was your prediction in C correct? Now read the entire passage carefully. Then answer the questions on page 14.**

Factors of success. Successful readers read fluently. To be fluent, you should be able to read 200 words per minute with at least 70 percent comprehension. In this chapter, see if you can achieve this goal. Achieving the goal will contribute to your success.

A Restaurant for Change

1 Jamie Oliver wants to change peoples' lives and he is using food to do it. Oliver, a chef, is well-known for sharing his secrets of cooking **healthy** food through his magazine, cookbooks, and television shows. He is also
5 changing lives through his Italian restaurant, Fifteen.

2 Fifteen started in London, England, as a place to train young adults to work in a kitchen. Oliver's idea was to create a professional **kitchen** that can help young people get a fresh start and a chance to become professional chefs.

3 10 Every September, a new group of 18- to 24-year-olds start work at Fifteen. When **they** start, they are usually not **qualified** for a restaurant job, but that will change quickly. In the 12 months
15 of training, the student chefs study cooking at college and get **hands-on** training at the restaurant. Besides learning kitchen skills, they learn the importance of using fresh **ingredients** and how to create their own **recipes**.

20 And their education doesn't stop with preparing and **serving** food. The students also learn how to manage money and deal with difficult customers. Overall, the program **encourages** them to believe in themselves and enables them to look forward to a future in the restaurant business.

4 The restaurant's name, Fifteen, comes from the number of students the
25 restaurant had when it started in 2002. Today, Oliver has three of these restaurants, and a few hundred students have finished the program. Around 90 percent of the graduates are still working in the food industry. Some own restaurants or work in some of the best kitchens around the world. Others are now starring in their own TV shows. They're all great examples of what young
30 people can do if they're given the opportunity and support.

Reading Comprehension
Check Your Understanding

A **Choose the correct answers for the following questions.**

1 Jamie Oliver _____ the Fifteen restaurant.
   a is a chef at
   b is the owner of
   c was a student at

2 Oliver uses Fifteen to help young people _____.
   a eat healthy food   b find jobs   c become rich

3 In lines 12–13, *When they start, they are usually*..., who does **they** refer to?
   a students at Fifteen   b TV chefs   c customers

4 Today, most Fifteen graduates are working in the _____ industry.
   a building   b education   c food

B **Number these events (1–4) in the order they happen.**

a _____ The student chefs graduate from their training.
b _____ The student chefs get hands-on training at a top restaurant.
c _____ In September, a new group of 18- to 24-year-olds start work.
d _____ The student chefs use their training to find jobs.

Critical Thinking

C **Discuss the following questions with a partner.**

1 Jamie Oliver started Fifteen to help young people get a fresh start in their lives. How could restaurant training make a young person's life better?

2 How does learning to manage money and difficult customers help someone in the restaurant business?

Vocabulary Comprehension
Words in Context

A **Complete each sentence with the best answer. The words in blue are from the passage.**

1 Qualified people are usually _____ to work.
   a trained   b not trained

2 The café near my home serves _____.
   a good chefs   b delicious food

3 Which of these are ingredients?
   a forks and spoons   b carrots and tomatoes

4 Since this is hands-on training, you'll need to _____.
   a travel to the place   b use your computer

5 Our English teacher encourages us _____.
   a to watch movies in English   b not to do our homework

6 Some examples of healthy foods are _____.
   a french fries and potato chips   b fruits and vegetables

7 You use a recipe to learn how a food _____.

    a tastes   **b** is made

8 Javier is _____ in the kitchen right now.

    a taking a shower   **b** cooking lunch

B **Answer the following questions. Then share your ideas with a partner.**

1 How would you encourage someone to speak English?

2 What things do you find in a kitchen?

3 What do you do to keep healthy?

4 What places do you know that serve good food?

A **The words in the chart below are all in the passage on page 13. Match these words with their antonyms from the box.**

| unhealthy | discourage | easy | ~~dislike~~ | rest | free |

		Antonym
1	like	*dislike*
2	difficult	
3	work	
4	healthy	
5	encourage	
6	busy	

B **Complete the sentences with the words from A. You might have to change the form of the word.**

1 You shouldn't eat so much _____ food.

2 Tonight's homework was very _____. I finished it in a few minutes.

3 You look tired. You should go and _____ for a while.

4 You should not let a small problem _____ you from reaching your goals.

5 I really _____ that girl. She's always so rude.

6 I didn't have lunch as I was _____ in the afternoon.

Vocabulary Skill
Antonyms

An antonym is a word that means the opposite of another word. Sometimes, antonyms are very different words, for example, *light* and *dark*, *true* and *false*. Other times, antonyms are made by adding or changing prefixes or suffixes, for example, *happy* and *unhappy*, *careless* and *careful*. One good way to increase your vocabulary is to learn antonyms.

CHAPTER 2 Let's Make Blueberry Muffins!

Before You Read
Famous Treats

A **Think about answers to the following questions.**

1 Can you name the desserts above? Have you ever eaten them?
2 What are your favorite desserts? Can you make them at home?

B **Discuss your answers with a partner.**

Reading Skill
Scanning

> Scanning is looking through a passage for information you need. For example, most people do not read a newspaper from beginning to end. They scan the headlines to find what they want to read. This saves time because you only read the information you want.

A **Scan the passage on the next page. Then answer the following questions.**

1 Find the list of things you need to make blueberry muffins. How many different ingredients are needed? _____
2 How many steps are there in making blueberry muffins? _____

B **Which step of the recipe uses each of these things? Scan the passage again and write the number of the step.**

1	salt	_____	**3**	egg	_____
2	blueberries	_____	**4**	cooking spray	_____

C **Now read the entire passage carefully. Then answer the questions on page 18.**

Let's Make Blueberry Muffins!

Muffins are pastries[1] that were first popular in England, Germany, and America in the 1800s. Today, muffins can be both sweet and savory.[2] Most people add fruit and vegetables to add flavor. These muffins are full of juicy blueberries and make a delicious breakfast meal.

Here's what you need:
1½ cups all-purpose flour
2 teaspoons baking powder
½ teaspoon salt
¾ cup white sugar
¼ cup butter
⅓ cup milk
1 large egg
2 teaspoons vanilla extract
1 cup fresh blueberries.

Makes 8 muffins
a muffin tin
an electric mixer
cooking spray

Step 1: Get the oven ready. _____
5   Heat the oven to 400ºF (200°C) and **spray** the muffin tin with cooking spray.

Step 2: Mix the dry ingredients. _____
In a large bowl, **mix** the flour, baking powder, salt, and 1/2 cup sugar together with a fork. When the ingredients are mixed well, make a hole in the center.

Step 3: Brown the butter. _____
10 **Melt** the butter in a pan over medium heat. When the butter melts, use a spoon to stir it. The butter will start to brown and smell nutty. When this happens, take the butter away from the stove.

Step 4: Make the batter. _____
Pour the butter and the milk into the hole you made in the flour. Mix everything together with the electric mixer. **Add** the egg and keep mixing. Then, add the vanilla. Don't mix the batter
15 too much. A few lumps are OK. Add the blueberries and use a spoon to stir. Be careful not to squish[3] the blueberries.

Step 5: Get ready to **bake**. _____
Pour the batter into each section of the muffin tin. Sprinkle[4] the remaining sugar over each muffin.

Step 6: Bake it! _____
20 Bake for about 16 to 20 minutes. The tops of the muffins will be golden brown. **Check** that they're done by inserting a toothpick into the middle of the muffin. If it comes out with a few (quite dry) crumbs, they're ready. Let the muffins **cool** in the tin for a few minutes before serving.

---

[1] A **pastry** is a kind of sweet food made of flour, butter, and water, and baked in the oven.
[2] **Savory** food tastes salty or spicy, not sweet.
[3] If you **squish** something, you press down on it, breaking it.
[4] If you **sprinkle** something on something else, you put small pieces of it on the other thing.

Reading Comprehension
Check Your Understanding

A **Choose the correct answers for the following questions.**

1 Which of these is NOT used in making blueberry muffins?
   a bacon   **b** butter   **c** blueberries

2 Which ingredient is melted?
   a salt   **b** butter   **c** vanilla

3 What ingredient goes on top of the muffins before baking?
   a baking powder   **b** vanilla   **c** sugar

4 How long does it take to make the muffins from start to finish?
   a less than 16–20 mins   **b** 16–20 mins   **c** more than 16–20 mins

B **Number the actions from the recipe in the correct order.**

a _____ Melt the butter in a pan over medium heat.

b _____ Add the blueberries and use a spoon to stir.

c _____ Put the muffin tin in the oven.

d _____ Spray the muffin tin with cooking spray.

e _____ Mix the flour, baking powder, salt, and ½ cup sugar.

f _____ Put a little sugar on top of the muffins.

Critical Thinking

C **Discuss the following questions with a partner.**

1 What makes blueberry muffins healthy? What makes them unhealthy?

2 How would you change this recipe to make it healthier?

Vocabulary Comprehension
Words in Context

A **Complete the following sentences with the correct words from the box. The words are from the passage.**

add	bake	cool	check
melt	mix	pour	spray

1 You _____ an apple pie.

2 You _____ the answer to a question.

3 You _____ water into a glass.

4 You _____ a wall with paint.

5 You _____ yellow and red to get orange.

6 You _____ chocolate over a fire.

7 You _____ sugar to something to make it sweeter.

8 You wait for hot soup to _____ before you drink it.

B **Answer the following questions, then discuss your answers with a partner. The words in blue are from the passage.**

1 What else can be melted?
2 How can you check if something is cooked properly?
3 What can you add to a dish to make it taste better?

A **Look at the list of irregular verbs below. Write the simple past tense in the chart. Use your dictionary to help you. Can you think of two more?**

Vocabulary Skill
Irregular Past Tense Verbs

Base form	Simple past	Base form	Simple past
break		have	
bring		keep	
buy		know	
come		lose	
cut		put	
do		ride	
eat		spread	
feel		take	
get			
go			

Regular verbs are formed in the past tense by adding -ed to the end of the verb; for example, *play/played*, *watch/watched*. Irregular verbs are not formed in this way; for example, *shut/shut*, *break/broke*. Many irregular verbs are very common, so it is important to know them.

B **Compare your list with a partner's. Do you notice any patterns in how any of these verbs are formed?**

C **Complete the following sentences with the correct form of the words from A.**

1 Ken _____ a chocolate cake to my party. It was delicious!
2 Can I use your glass? Mine _____ yesterday.
3 Maria _____ into the kitchen to get something to drink.
4 My mother _____ me a new cell phone so I would call her more often.
5 I collected over 100 old newspapers off the street and I _____ them to the recycling center.
6 I _____ three pieces of candy last night. It's difficult to eat only one!

Learning new vocabulary can be fun. Learning new vocabulary can be one of the most enjoyable parts of becoming a good reader. In addition to the vocabulary that is explicitly taught in this chapter, are there other words related to this topic that you would like to learn?

Real Life Skill
Reading Food Labels

In many countries, food labels give important information about what is in the foods we buy. Reading and understanding the labels can help you to eat more healthily.

A **The words in blue are sometimes found on food labels. Write each word next to the correct definition.**

The ingredients of onion soup are onions, butter, water, salt, and pepper.
Minerals like calcium are important for your body.
Additives are used to change the color or taste of a food.
Oranges contain vitamin C.
This bread contains preservatives so it stays fresh for a longer time.
That piece of cake had 129 calories in it.

1 things that your body needs, such as iron   _____
2 B, C, and D are examples of these   _____
3 these keep a food from going bad   _____
4 things added to a food   _____
5 the things used to make a food   _____
6 units of energy in your food   _____

B **Read the labels for these food bars and complete the following sentences.**

No added sugar No additives	The taste you love...	A complete meal—only 200 calories
High protein for an active life **Power up**	**Chocoblock**	**SLIM QUICK**
Lots of vitamins and minerals, and all the energy you need!	**Ingredients: sugar, honey, butter, cocoa, peanuts, salt, preservatives**	Strawberry-yogurt flavor Fiber and protein to help you feel full longer—low in calories to help you lose weight faster!

1 A seven-year-old child would eat _____
   because _____ .
2 A person trying to lose weight would eat _____
   because _____ .
3 A football player would eat _____
   because _____ .

What do you think?

1 Do you think it is healthier to eat at home or at a restaurant? Why?
2 Should children and older people eat the same foods? How should our food choices change as we age?
3 Vegetarians (people who don't eat meat) are becoming more common in some countries. Why do you think this is?

Inventions

Getting Ready

A Match the letters of the following inventions to the correct pictures above.

a _____ camera	**b** _____ desktop computer	**c** _____ dishwasher
d _____ microwave	**e** _____ smart phone	**f** _____ vacuum cleaner

B When do you think these things were invented? Write the numbers from
1 (first invented) to 6 (last invented) next to the names in **A**.

C Why do you think these inventions were successful? Discuss with a partner.

Before You Read
"Watson"

A Think about answers to the following questions.

1 Look at the photograph on the next page. You are going to read about Watson. Who, or what, is Watson?

2 Have you heard of the television show *Jeopardy*? If not, what other game shows do you know?

B Discuss your answers with a partner.

Reading Skill
Reading for Details

When we read for details, we read every word carefully and think carefully about the meaning. It is usually best to read for details when we are looking for information in a part of a passage—for example, when answering questions for a test.

A Read the following sentences. Then scan the first paragraph of the passage on the next page for the information. Check (✔) true (T) or false (F) for each sentence. If the sentence is false, change it to make it true.

		T	F
1	Ken Jennings and Brad Rutter had never been on *Jeopardy!* before.		
2	This was the first time the men played against Watson.		
3	Watson often got answers wrong.		
4	The men and Watson competed against each other in 2010.		

B Now read the entire passage carefully. Then answer the questions on page 24.

Compliment your classmates. When you compliment your classmates you help to create a positive learning environment. During this chapter, watch your classmates closely and identify positive things that they do. Did they score well on the comprehension test? Did someone read very well in one of the chapters? How can you compliment each other on improved reading performance?

Computer Beats Champs

1 In 2011, on the popular American TV quiz show, *Jeopardy!*, two **champions** competed against a brand new **opponent**. Both Ken Jennings and Brad Rutter had won millions of dollars on *Jeopardy!* Jennings once won 74 games in a row, the most ever. Then Rutter **beat** him in a tournament and set a new record for the most money won

on *Jeopardy!* Their new opponent, Watson, had never appeared on the game show and had only played practice games before, in which he often got answers wrong.

2 However, Watson isn't human. *He*, or rather *it*, is a **machine**, a **wonder** of technology made by researchers at IBM. In the game, Watson used math to decide on an answer. When a question was read out, Watson was immediately given the same question in electronic form. It analyzed the question and searched its memory bank—about the same as one million books of information—for possible answers. It then narrowed the options down to one answer. If Watson felt around 75 percent **confident** about the answer, it would answer the question.

3 The way Watson thinks is very different from the way humans think. People often make decisions by listening to their emotions and feelings, even if they are unsure of the answer. As a computer, Watson couldn't do this. People also watch and listen to those around them. Watson was not able to "listen" to the wrong answers given by his **competitors**. In one question, Jennings answered the question incorrectly and Watson later answered with the same wrong answer.

4 Watson also made silly mistakes. In a question in the category *U.S. Cities*, Watson incorrectly answered *Toronto*, even though the city of Toronto is in Canada. An IBM researcher said Watson got **confused** because it saw in its memory bank that the U.S. is often called *America*. Toronto is considered a North American city, so that was the answer that Watson gave.

5 Still, Watson defeated his human opponents somewhat easily and received the $1 million prize. The other players also won money for participating in the special game. Everyone left the game happy, as each player was earning money for a different charity.

Reading Comprehension
Check Your Understanding

A **Choose the correct answers for the following questions.**

1 Ken Jennings and Brad Rutter played a special game against a

_____.

   a man   **b** researcher   **c** computer

2 Watson used _____ to answer the questions.

   a feelings   **b** paper   **c** math

3 Watson made a mistake because it thought the question was about

cities in _____.

   a the U.S.   **b** Canada   **c** America

4 The money the players won in the game went to _____.

   a charity   **b** *Jeopardy!*   **c** Watson

B **In which paragraph (1–5) of the passage can you find the following information? Write the number. You may use any number more than once.**

   a Watson is a machine that uses math to answer questions.   _____

   b Watson sometimes gets confused.   _____

   c Ken Jennings and Brad Rutter are *Jeopardy!* champions.   _____

   d Watson won, but everyone received money.   _____

   e Watson makes decisions in a different way from humans.   _____

Critical Thinking

C **Discuss the following questions with a partner.**

1 Watson beat two very smart men. Why do you think Watson won?

2 Which is smarter: humans or machines? Why do you think so?

Vocabulary Comprehension
Definitions

A **Match each word with its definition. The words in blue are from the passage.**

1 _____ beat   **a** not able to understand something

2 _____ competitor   **b** to feel sure of something

3 _____ confused   **c** a person who is trying to win a competition

4 _____ champion   **d** an amazing thing

5 _____ wonder   **e** the person you are competing against

6 _____ machine   **f** winner

7 _____ confident   **g** win against another person or team

8 _____ opponent   **h** a car, a clock, a mixer, etc.

B **Complete the following sentences with words in blue from A. You might have to change the form of the word.**

1 I am a good English student, but math _____ me.

2 I played games with my friend last night. I _____ her every time!

3 In the Olympics, the _____ are usually the best in their country.

4 Mary said she was not _____ that she would pass the test.

5 Look at that beautiful rainbow. Isn't it a(n) _____ of nature?

6 Nowadays, people are worried that their jobs may be replaced by

_____ .

7 Even though his _____ was very good, Sam won the match and became tennis _____ .

A **Match the word parts in the box to the correct prefix. Write them below.**

-municate	-nect	-pare	-fort	-tain	-mon

Com-
communicate

Con-

Vocabulary Skill
The Prefixes *com-* and *con-*

Com- and *con-* are prefixes that mean *with* or *together*. Remembering what these prefixes mean can help you to understand more words.

B **Match the following definitions with the correct words from A.**

1 to join or link together _____

2 normal; ordinary _____

3 to have, include _____

4 to talk to and understand others _____

5 to look at how two or more things are the same or different _____

6 to help someone feel better when something bad happens _____

C **Complete the following sentences with words from A. You might have to change the form of the word.**

1 I had to _____ my son when his cat died.

2 This soup already _____ salt, but I added a little more.

3 In England, "John" is a very _____ name for a man.

4 Before you buy new shoes, you should _____ prices in several different stores.

5 Deaf people _____ with others by making signs with their hands.

6 We cut a door in this wall, so now the kitchen is _____ to the dining room.

CHAPTER 2 The Most Useful Inventions

Before You Read
Useful Inventions

A Look at the list of useful inventions below. Work with a partner to add three more to the list.

> _____ the telephone _____ the Internet
> _____ the car _____ _____
> _____ the airplane _____ _____
> _____ paper _____ _____

B Rank the inventions from 1 (most useful) to 8 (least useful). Discuss your answers with a partner.

Reading Skill
Scanning

> When we scan a text we look for specific information, for example, names and dates. We move our eyes quickly over the page, and we do not read the information that we are not looking for. In Chapter 2 of Unit 1 we used scanning to find information in a recipe, and we mentioned that scanning is useful when taking tests. It is also very useful for getting information from websites.

A Look quickly at the web forum (an online discussion board) on the next page. When did each writer post their message? Match each date with the writer's name.

1 April 13 _____   a Kazuo
2 April 14 _____   b Cindy
3 April 15 _____   c Jorge

B Which invention did each writer think is the most important? Match each invention with the writer's name.

1 air conditioner _____   a Kazuo
2 electricity _____   b Cindy
3 the Internet _____   c Jorge

C Read the entire discussion carefully. Then answer the questions on page 28.

> **Internal and external rewards.** Our rewards can be both internal and external. Make a list of three internal and three external rewards. Make sure that you reward yourself with both types. For example, every time you get all the questions right, you could give yourself a treat (external). You should also feel good that you've improved (internal).

TALK ABOUT IT

Forum ⟶ Science Stuff ⟶ The Most Useful Inventions

TOPIC: THE MOST USEFUL INVENTIONS

The other day, my friends and I had a **discussion** about the most useful invention of all time. There were many good ideas—the train, the car, and the airplane. They're all useful, but they were not my choices. For an everyday, useful invention, I **vote** for the air conditioner. I live in Taipei, and **during** the summer the **temperature** can 5 be 35 degrees Celsius or higher. It's so hot! I'm not joking when I say that, without an air conditioner, people here couldn't work or study. The weather is so hot that it can make you feel unwell if you don't drink enough water and get enough rest. What do you guys think is the most useful invention of all time? 10

Posted by Cindy Wu on Saturday, April 13

I don't know if I agree with you, Cindy. For me, the most useful invention of all time is **surely** the Internet. We can now reach people and do business faster. I own a clothing store in Mexico City, and there's a lot of competition. I also have a website. Now, 15 people from all over the world can buy my clothing. With emails, I can **keep in touch** with friends and family in Mexico and around the world. It's faster than usual mail, and it's cheaper than using the phone!

Posted by Jorge on Sunday, April 14 20

Jorge, I also think that the Internet is **useful**. But, in my **opinion**, there is an "invention" that is even more important, and that's electricity. Of course, this isn't a man-made invention, but without people like Benjamin Franklin and Alessandro Volta, we wouldn't have learned how to use it. And without electricity, many of the 25 world's most important modern inventions would not work.

Posted by Kazuo on Monday, April 15

Reading Comprehension
Check Your Understanding

A **Choose the correct answers for the following questions.**

1 For Cindy, the air conditioner is the most useful because _____.
   a her apartment doesn't smell very good
   b she lives in a very hot place
   c she often gets sick

2 Jorge says that the Internet helps him to _____.
   a sell air conditioners to people around the world
   b keep in touch with family and friends
   c use the telephone more cheaply

3 Kazuo thinks electricity is the most useful invention because _____.
   a many machines cannot work without it
   b Benjamin Franklin invented it
   c it isn't really man-made

4 Who is most likely to agree that communication is the most important?
   a Cindy   b Jorge   c Kazuo

B **Answer the following questions by checking (✔) Cindy (C), Jorge (J), or Kazuo (K).**

Who . . . ?	C	J	K
1 chose an invention that people didn't make			
2 mentioned trains, cars, and planes			
3 sells clothing			
4 talked to friends about the topic			
5 has a website			

Critical Thinking

C **Discuss the following questions with a partner.**

1 Which of the three writers in the reading passage do you most agree with?
2 Do you ever post messages on websites? If so, which ones? If not, why not?

Vocabulary Comprehension
Words in Context

A **Complete each statement with the best answer. The words in blue are from the passage.**

1 During a discussion, people _____.
   a do their own work   b share their ideas

2 If you do something during class, you do it _____.
   a at the same time as the class   b a little before the class

3 There is surely a way to solve the problem. We should _____.
   a give up   b keep on trying

4 I asked for your opinion because I want to know how you _____.
   a did it   b felt about it

5 When we keep in touch with someone, we _____.
   a compliment them   b communicate with them

6 Which of these can people vote for?

    a a president   **b** their parents

7 The temperature in this room is _____ .

    a 35 centimeters   **b** 22 degrees Celsius

8 English is a very useful language because _____ .

    a many people speak it   **b** it is very difficult

B **Complete the paragraph with words in blue from A. You might have to change the form of the word.**

It was so hot yesterday! I think the **(1)** _____ was nearly 40 degrees Celsius. In the office where I work, we have air conditioning, but it isn't very strong, so it's not very **(2)** _____ . Instead, we held most of our team **(3)** _____ at a café nearby. The weather report said that it would **(4)** _____ cool down next week, so hopefully, things won't stay like this for long.

A **Look at the words in the box. Add the suffixes *-ful* and *-less* to each one to make positive and negative antonyms, then write them on the correct line. Can you add any more words?**

> use   care   thought   help   rest

Positive: _____

Negative: _____

B **Match the following definitions with the correct words from A. Be careful; not all of the words will be used.**

1 thinking of others   _____

2 moving around a lot; not relaxed   _____

3 not paying attention when doing something   _____

4 not able to do anything in a bad situation   _____

5 calm, peaceful, relaxed   _____

6 having no purpose   _____

C **Complete the following sentences with the words from A.**

1 Ming was very _____ and added salt to his coffee instead of sugar.

2 Be very _____ not to mix the eggs too quickly.

3 We felt so _____ when the other team beat us. There was nothing we could do.

4 This knife is _____! It doesn't cut anything.

5 That was very _____ of you to talk about Carol's weight. You know she's very sensitive about it!

6 Aki doesn't sleep well. He was so _____ that he got up four times last night.

Vocabulary Skill
The Suffixes *-ful* and *-less*

> The suffixes *-ful* and *-less* have opposite meanings. When *-ful* is added to a word it means *with* or *full of*. When *-less* is added it means *without*. Some root words can have both suffixes added to make adjectives that are antonyms. For example, *useful* describes something that is helpful and has a use. *Useless* describes something that is not helpful or does not have a use.

Real Life Skill

Dictionary Skills:
Identifying Parts of
Speech

In English, the same
word can be used as
several different parts
of speech, with different
meanings; for example,
work can mean *to do
a job* when used as a
verb. When used as a
noun, it means *a job*.

A **Look at the dictionary abbreviations for the parts of speech below. Read the three examples for each one, then add two more examples of your own.**

n. (noun)	Jamie, bowl, machine, _____ , _____
v. (verb)	fill, support, invite, _____ , _____
adj. (adjective)	simple, healthy, curious, _____ , _____
adv. (adverb)	surely, carefully, happily, _____ , _____
prep. (preposition)	during, after, in, _____ , _____

B **Look at the dictionary entries below, then read the paragraph that follows. (Circle) the correct abbreviation in the paragraph to show the part of speech for each word.**

cool	/kuːl/	*v.* to make the temperature of something go down; *adj.* having a low temperature
cover	/kʌvə/	*n.* something that fits on top of a can, jar, etc; *v.* to put something over another thing
form	/fɔːm/	*n.* the shape of something; *v.* to change the shape of something
joke	/dʒəʊk/	*n.* words that make people laugh; *v.* to say something to make people laugh

Dear Diary,

Today was a nice, cool **1 (v. / adj.)** day! Anna and I decided to sit outside her house and look up at the sky. We saw forms **2 (v. / n.)** of animals in the clouds. I made Anna laugh **3 (n. / v.)** when I said I could see her up there, too. Later, we went into the kitchen as there was a nice smell **4 (n. / v.)**. Anna's mom had put two apple pies out to cool **5 (v. / adj.)**. In the evening after dinner, we each had a slice of pie. It was delicious!

What do you think?

1 What do you think were some of the very first inventions?

2 Who are some famous inventors? Would you like to be an inventor?

3 What are some inventions that might be made in the future?

Studying Abroad

Getting Ready

Discuss the following questions with a partner.

1   Do you like to travel? What countries have you visited?
2   Have you ever studied in another country? Did you like it?
3   Why do you think people want to study abroad?

CHAPTER 1 Want to Study Abroad?

Before You Read
Planning to Study

A Look at these reasons for studying abroad. Add your own ideas to the list.

> experience life in a different country
> make friends
> go sightseeing
> be able to speak English all day
> get a better job
> get ready to live abroad
>
> _____
>
> _____

B Which of these reasons would you study abroad for? Discuss your answers with a partner.

Reading Skill
Using Subheadings to Predict Content

Sometimes passages are divided into paragraphs that have subheadings. We can use our knowledge of the topic and these subheadings to predict some of the ideas that may be in the passage.

A Look at the passage on the next page. Read only the title and the subheadings of the four main paragraphs. What ideas do you think will be in each paragraph? Fill in the chart below with your predictions.

Subheading	Ideas
Why do it?	
Making the right choice	
Getting ready to go	
Once you are there	

B Skim each of the four main paragraphs. Are any of the ideas in your chart the same as the ideas in the passage?

C Now read the entire passage carefully. Then answer the questions on page 34.

Want to Study Abroad?

Choose TraveLingua!

Every year, thousands of students choose to
5 study **abroad** for the summer— whether it's for six months, a year, or even longer. Many people find the
10 **experience** of studying abroad very **exciting**, but also very scary. Let TraveLingua give you some advice.

15 Why do it?

Living in another country will help you learn a language and learn about another **culture**. You will see the world in a new way and learn more about yourself. Studying abroad is also **excellent** training for the working world. Many companies want employees who speak a second language or who have experienced living or working in another country.

20 Making the right choice

To choose the right country or school, ask yourself these questions: For how long do I want to study abroad? Do I want to live with a host family,[1] with roommates, or alone? How much can I afford to pay? If you aren't sure how to answer these questions, our experienced staff can help!

Getting ready to go

25 Based on our experience, it's best to get your passport and visa[2] early! Before you go, learn as much of the language as you can and read about the customs of your host country. Also, talk with people who have experience studying abroad. And call the school to **make sure** someone can meet you when you get there. Make sure to bring some local money and a credit card.

Once you are there

30 Be curious and open to meeting new people and having new experiences. Don't expect to always be **comfortable**. After the first few weeks it's usual to feel a little homesick.[3] You'll **miss** your family and friends. Remember that it takes time to get used to a new place with new customs. Talk to your new friends and write about your feelings. Try to keep in touch with the people back home.

TraveLingua helps you get started on your journey by doing all this, and more. Choose us as your travel
35 partner, and we'll be sure to get you where you want to go!

---

[1] A **host family** is a family that students live with while they're abroad.
[2] A **visa** is the paper or stamp in your passport that lets you enter and stay in another country.
[3] If you feel **homesick**, you miss your home, family, and friends while traveling.

Reading Comprehension
Check Your Understanding

A **Choose the correct answers for the following questions.**

1 Travelingua is a company that helps students _____.
   a get into a school
   b meet people abroad
   c prepare to go abroad

2 The advertisement does NOT ask you to think about _____.
   a who to live with
   b how much you can pay
   c what the food is like

3 The advertisement suggests that you take _____ with you.
   a a credit card   b extra pencils   c books

4 Many students will feel _____ after a few weeks.
   a afraid   b happy   c homesick

B **What should a new student do? Number the steps from 1–4.**

a ____ Talk to your new friends and write about your feelings.

b ____ Phone the school to ask for someone to meet you.

c ____ Get your visa.

d ____ Decide where you want to go and for how long you want to study abroad.

Critical Thinking

C **Discuss the following questions with a partner.**

1 What kinds of people might use TraveLingua?

2 What advice can you add to the *Getting ready to go* and *Once you are there* sections of the advertisement?

Vocabulary Comprehension
Odd Word Out

A **For each group of words, ⬭ circle ⬭ the word that does not belong. The words in blue are from the passage.**

1	traditions	culture	kitchen
2	experience	knowledge	competition
3	homesick	comfortable	relaxed
4	exciting	interesting	funny
5	sick	great	excellent
6	opinion	abroad	overseas
7	make sure	work	check
8	dislike	hate	miss

> **Don't be afraid to make mistakes.** Mistakes are a natural part of learning. Everyone makes mistakes, so don't be embarrassed if you make one in class. Motivated learners are willing to take risks and not fear getting something wrong—that's how you can learn what's right!

B Complete the sentences with the words in blue from A.

1 The _____ here is very different. In my country, it's polite to leave some food on your plate.
2 Please _____ to switch off the lights when you leave the room.
3 I really _____ my family. I'm going to call them tonight.
4 This chair is so _____ that I'm falling asleep in it!

A Look at how some compound words are made.

Vocabulary Skill
Compound Words

Some join two nouns together to form one word:

> room + mate = roommate

Some put two nouns together to talk about a single thing:

> air + conditioner = air conditioner

Others join adjectives and nouns together to make one word or a hyphenated word:

> home + sick = homesick   man + made = man-made

Compound words are formed by putting two words together to form a new word—for example, *man-made*. Sometimes compound words are hyphenated. Sometime they are not.

B Match a word from the box with the nouns and adjectives listed below to form compound words.

> sick   book   time   credit   pass   water

1 _____ card
2 part-_____
3 _____ fountain
4 note _____
5 _____word
6 home_____

C Complete the sentences with the compound words from B.

1 Excuse me, can I pay for this with my _____?
2 I'm very thirsty. Where is the nearest _____?
3 The first time I went abroad, I got _____ after only one week.
4 He works _____ at the school cafe so he can earn extra money.
5 You shouldn't share your computer _____ with anyone.
6 Can I have some paper to write on? I left my _____ at home.

CHAPTER 2 My Travel Journal

Before You Read
Writing a Journal

A Scan the travel journal on the next page. Look only at the title, the subheadings, and the photographs. Then answer the following questions.

1 Who wrote the travel journal? _____

2 Where did she travel to? _____

3 How long was she traveling?

    a more than one month   **b** less than one month

B Discuss your answers in **A**, and the following questions, with a partner.

1 Would you enjoy reading someone's travel journal? Why, or why not?

2 Do you keep a travel journal, or would you like to? Why, or why not?

Reading Skill
Reading for Details

> Reading for details is especially useful when we need to get information from one part of a larger passage. We can scan the passage to find out which part we need to read more carefully, and then look for specific details.

A Read the following sentences, then scan the second paragraph of the journal on the next page. Check (✔) the three things Maria wrote about on October 20.

1 ☐ It is difficult for her to talk to her classmates.

2 ☐ She doesn't know how to take the bus.

3 ☐ She is making lots of friends.

4 ☐ She can't understand her teacher.

5 ☐ Her English is improving very slowly.

6 ☐ She had trouble understanding someone on the bus.

B Scan the third paragraph of the journal for the following information. Check (✔) the three things Maria wrote about on October 27.

1 ☐ She wrote for the student newspaper.

2 ☐ She met a French woman.

3 ☐ She talked about her experiences in the United States.

4 ☐ She met a Japanese man.

5 ☐ She walked around the city.

6 ☐ She went to a party.

C Now read the entire journal carefully. Then answer the questions on page 38.

Your teacher is a role model. Listen to your teacher share his or her personal reasons for learning English. If your teacher is a native speaker of English, find out how your teacher improves his or her English.

Maria

My Travel Journal

September 13

1 Hi Journal! It's me, Maria! I arrived in New York City two weeks ago. I am writing this **journal** for one of my classes. My teacher says it is a good way for me to **practice** writing in English and to write about my experiences here in the United
5 States. So far, I like New York and my school. I have three classes a day. Most of my classmates come from Japan, Korea, Poland, Germany, and Brazil. There aren't many Italian students, so I have to use English most of the time. I am learning a lot! I am living in student housing, and I have my own comfortable room.

October 20

2 10 My English is hopeless! I was on the bus this morning and a man spoke to me, but I **hardly** understood him. I was so **embarrassed**. Why is my English **improving** so slowly? I want to make **lots of** American friends, but this isn't happening so easily. I feel **shy**, and it is hard for me to talk to people, even my classmates! I like them, but sometimes I can't understand them very well. I'm feeling homesick. I miss my
15 friends and family.

October 27

3 I went to a school party last Friday and it was **awesome**. I talked with a Japanese man named Kenji and a Polish woman named Anna. We talked about our countries' customs and our experiences in the States so far. We are going to walk around the
20 city together this weekend. Also, Kenji wants me to write for the student newspaper here at school. Maybe things are getting better!

Reading Comprehension
Check Your Understanding

A Choose the correct answers for the following questions.

1 Whose idea was it for Maria to keep a journal?
   a her classmates'   **b** her teacher's   **c** Kenji's

2 The students in Maria's class are _____ .
   a mostly Polish
   b all Japanese and Italian
   c from different countries

3 Why did Maria get embarrassed?
   a She took the wrong bus.
   b She couldn't understand someone.
   c She cried in class.

4 At the end of October, Maria was feeling _____ .
   a ready to go home
   b depressed and homesick
   c better than before

B Number these events (1–4) in the order they happened.

a _____ A man spoke to her on the bus.
b _____ Maria arrived in New York.
c _____ Maria started keeping a travel journal.
d _____ She went to a party.

Critical Thinking

C Discuss the following questions with your partner.

1 Do you think it's better to study English with students who are from many different countries or who are all from the same country? Why?

2 How can we learn from our mistakes when learning a new language?

Vocabulary Comprehension
Words in Context

A Complete each statement with the best answer. The words in blue are from the passage.

1 If Jin-Song's friends think his shoes are awesome, they _____ .
   a really like them   **b** don't like them

2 Because I have lots of money, I _____ .
   a can't buy too many things   **b** can give some to my friends

3 I think my English is improving because _____ .
   a I can understand American movies now
   b I try not to speak in class

4 Jun was really embarrassed during class because she _____ .
   a forgot to bring her homework   **b** got an A on the test

5 You need to practice playing tennis by _____.

  a getting enough sleep   **b** hitting lots of balls

6 Sandra uses a journal to _____.

  a write about things that happen to her   **b** read the news

7 I can hardly hear you. Can you speak a little _____?

  a softer   **b** louder

8 Yuki is really shy. She _____ talking to people she doesn't know.

  a likes   **b** dislikes

B **Answer the following questions, then discuss your answers with a partner. The words in blue are from the passage.**

1 What places do you know that have lots of trees?

2 How do you practice English?

3 Which actor or actress do you think is awesome? Why do you think so?

4 How has your English improved in the past few years?

A **Look at the list of verbs below. Make adjectives that describe feelings by adding -ed. Write them in the chart. Can you think of any other words to add to the chart?**

Verb	Adjective
depress	*depressed*
embarrass	
excite	
tire	
worry	
interest	

B **Complete the paragraph below with adjectives from A. Some have more than one answer.**

Healthy Living Gym

Do you feel sad and **(1)** _____? Are you **(2)** _____ all the time? Are you **(3)** _____ about your health? You may not be getting enough exercise. Healthy Living Gym encourages you to come in and start exercising today. You'll feel **(4)** _____ about losing weight and looking great. Are you **(5)** _____? Don't be **(6)** _____! Come in today!

Vocabulary Skill

Adjectives Ending in -ed

Some adjectives that describe how we are feeling end in -ed. Most of these adjectives come from verbs with the same root word. For example, from the verb *interest* we can make the adjective *interested* by adding -ed. For verbs that end in *y*, we change the *y* to an *i* and add -ed; for example, *worry* becomes *worried*.

Real Life Skill

Writing an English Journal

Writing a journal is a good way to remember your thoughts and experiences, to keep a record of what you learn, and to practice your English writing skills. You can keep a journal of all your daily experiences, or about one subject such as travel, books you read, or how your studies are going.

A **Read the following tips for keeping a journal.**

- Use a notebook with lined paper that gives you lots of space for writing.
- Make sure to include the date every time you write in your journal.
- Write about things that are interesting or important to you.
- Try to make a regular time for writing in your journal—for example, three times a week after English class or every evening.
- Don't worry about grammar and spelling.
- Read your journal entry again before you give it to your teacher.

B **Now read this journal entry.**

Tuesday, October 15

Today, I finished reading an exciting book called *The Perfect Storm*. It was about a group of men on a fishing boat that sank in a very bad storm. The book talked about their families and friends, and it was a really sad story. I would like to see the movie that was made about this story. Tomorrow I will start reading a Harry Potter book.

C **Now write a journal entry about an interesting book or story that you have read.**

What do you think?

1 If you got homesick abroad, how would you make yourself feel better?
2 Think of five good things about studying abroad and tell your partner.
3 Do you know anyone who has studied abroad? How did their experience change them?

Fluency Strategy: SQ3R

SQ3R is a simple way to help you be a better, more fluent reader and to increase your reading comprehension. SQ3R stands for **Survey**, **Question**, **Read**, **Review**, **Recite**.

Survey

Survey is similar to the **A**—for *Activate prior knowledge*—in the **ACTIVE** approach to reading. When you survey a passage, you prepare yourself by skimming quickly through the passage. Read just the title, the headings, and the first sentence in each section of the passage. Look for and read words that are written in **bold** or *italics*. Look at any pictures and read any captions. Through the survey, you prepare yourself to read.

Look at these extracts from the passage on the next page, then go on to the Question section below.

The Freshman Fifteen
You may not have heard the words *freshman fifteen* before, but they are very important for students who are entering college. A *freshman* is a first-year college student.

Making the wrong choices

How to stay healthy

Question

Before you read the passage on the next page, ask yourself: *What do I want to learn as I read?* Write two or three questions that you hope to answer as you read.

1 _____
2 _____
3 _____

Read

After you have done the survey and question stages of **SQ3R**, you are ready to **read**. You should focus on comprehending the material, moving your eyes fluently through the passage.

Read *The Freshman Fifteen*. As you read, keep the 12 tips on pages 8 and 9 in mind. By combining these tips and **SQ3R**, you will improve your reading fluency.

The Freshman Fifteen

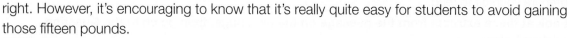

You may not have heard the words *freshman fifteen* before, but they are very important for students who are entering college. A *freshman* is a first-year college student.

5 And the *fifteen* refers to fifteen pounds—the fifteen pounds (about seven kilograms) of weight many American students will gain in their first year at college. There are a few reasons why first-year college students often

10 gain weight. The most common reason is that many college students just don't eat right. However, it's encouraging to know that it's really quite easy for students to avoid gaining those fifteen pounds.

Making the wrong choices

15 College kitchens serve many kinds of food. New students often gain weight because they are choosing to eat a lot of unhealthy food, especially when their parents are not around to advise them on what they should eat. Some students may also buy snacks to eat while they are studying. The average college student often stays up late at night, so he or she might eat a lot of fast food and drink a lot of soda because these things are easy to get at night. Furthermore,

20 college students often have less time for walking, running, and doing sports because they are busy with their schoolwork or other college activities.

How to stay healthy

However, if you're careful, you can avoid gaining the freshman fifteen. Here are some ideas for staying healthy at college:

25 • Eat only when you are hungry, not when you're bored.

• Fill half of your plate with vegetables.

• Don't eat desserts that are full of sugar; have some fruit after dinner instead.

• Try not to eat while you study, or keep healthy snacks like baby carrots nearby.

• Always eat at the dinner table and never in front of the TV or the computer.

30 • Choose water over sugary drinks.

• Try to get out of your room regularly for some fresh air and exercise.

Remember that the freshman fifteen can happen to anyone. Make a deal with your friends to try and eat healthy food together. Walking, running, and playing sports is always more fun with friends, too. Help each other eat right and stay fit, and you can have a happy and healthy

35 freshman year.

Review

After you have read the passage, you should **review** what you have read. This is the review stage of **SQ3R**. Review the questions that you asked yourself before reading.

A   Did you find answers to your questions on page 41? Write the answers below.

1   _____

2   _____

3   _____

B   **Choose the correct answers for the following questions.**

1   The *freshman fifteen* refers to _____.
   a   weight that high school students gain
   b   fifteen pounds of food that first-year students eat
   c   weight that first-year college students gain
   d   fifteen students who eat junk food

2   The purpose of this passage is to _____.
   a   get students ready to gain fifteen pounds
   b   sell healthy food to new students
   c   help new college students to stay healthy
   d   show the mistakes students make in their schoolwork

3   Which of these ideas about eating right is NOT mentioned in the passage?
   a   eating vegetables
   b   not eating unless you are hungry
   c   choosing fruit for dessert
   d   eating less red meat

4   What advice does the passage give about sports?
   a   Students should do sports with their friends.
   b   Students should study before doing sports.
   c   Students should join a sports team.
   d   Students should exercise less and study more.

5   Which of these ideas would the writer of the passage probably agree with?
   a   Gaining fifteen pounds just can't be avoided.
   b   Staying healthy is easier with friends' help.
   c   You should eat while you study.
   d   Some students can eat anything they want.

Recite

The final step of **SQ3R** is to **recite** what you have learned. The important thing is that you close your book and remember what you have read. You can recite what you've learned in different ways.

- If you are alone, write down the key information that you learned as you were reading.
- If you have a partner, talk to them about what you have read.

SELF CHECK

Answer the following questions.

1 Have you ever used the **SQ3R** method before?

☐ Yes ☐ No ☐ I'm not sure.

2 Do you think **SQ3R** is helpful? Why, or why not?

_____

_____

3 Will you practice **SQ3R** in your reading outside of English class?

_____

_____

4 Which of the six passages in units 1–3 did you enjoy most? Why?

_____

_____

5 Which of the six passages in units 1–3 was easiest? Which was most difficult? Why?

_____

_____

6 What have you read in English outside of class recently?

_____

_____

7 What distractions do you have when you read? What can you do to reduce those distractions?

_____

_____

8 How will you try to improve your reading fluency from now on?

_____

_____

Four Funny Inventions

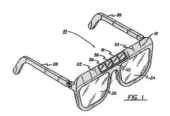

Time Temp Glasses

Have you always wanted to keep an eye on the time *and* temperature at the same time? Then you'll love the Time Temp Glasses! These special glasses show the time above your right eye and the temperature above your left eye. It is certainly easier than wearing a wristwatch, and you'll never have to guess the temperature again.

5

Alarm Fork

10 Do you eat too quickly? Do you eat too much? The Alarm Fork can help you. This special fork has two lights: one green and one red. When the green light is on, it's OK to take a bite of food. The fork *knows* when you take a bite, and the red light will go on. Then, you must wait for the green light to come on again before you take another bite. This will help you eat slowly and eat less as well!

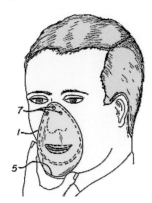

Smell This

15

How do you know when you have bad breath? Your friends probably don't want to tell you, and it's hard to smell the air that comes out of your own mouth. Now you can avoid embarrassment with the Smell This machine. It covers your nose and your mouth, so you can always smell your own breath. So does it smell nice…or do you need a piece of gum?

20

Crash Wing

Riding a motorcycle can be an awesome experience, but it can also be a dangerous one. Make your ride safer with the Crash Wing. This safety device is worn on your back like a backpack, with part of it attached to the motorcycle. If you are thrown from your bike, the Crash Wing opens, spreading

25

30 its wings. The wings lift you up into the air and help you float safely back to the ground. With Crash Wing, you can ride your motorcycle with confidence!

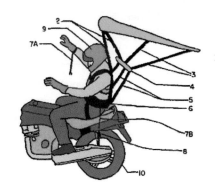

307 words   **Time taken** _____

Reading Comprehension

Choose the correct answers for the following questions.

1 Why did the writer choose to write about these four inventions?
  a They are all dangerous.
  b They are all very important.
  c They are all unusual.
  d They are all expensive.

2 Who would find the Time Temp Glasses most useful in their job?
  a a writer
  b a weather reporter
  c a doctor
  d a police officer

3 When using the Alarm Fork, the green light means _____ .
  a your food is ready to eat
  b your food is properly cooked
  c you can take another bite
  d you should wait to take another bite

4 People should use the Crash Wing to _____ .
  a carry birds on a motorcycle
  b stop their motorcycles from crashing
  c float through the air
  d keep safe when riding their motorcycles

5 Which invention should you use if you're trying to lose weight?
  a Time Temp Glasses
  b Alarm Fork
  c Smell This
  d Crash Wing

6 Which invention should you use before talking to people?
  a Time Temp Glasses
  b Alarm Fork
  c Smell This
  d Crash Wing

Turn to page 176 to record your reading fluency progress. First, find the vertical line that is closest to your reading rate. Next, how many of the six comprehension questions did you answer correctly? Find the point on the graph where your reading rate and your comprehension score meet. Mark that spot with a dot.
Which quadrant does the dot fall in? Your goal is to be a fluent reader and score in quadrant four.

Review Reading 2: My Working Holiday

Fluency Practice

Time yourself as you read through the passage. Write your time in the space at the bottom of the page. Then answer the questions on the next page.

Traveler's Corner Summer Edition

My Working Holiday

Would you like to go on a holiday, and earn money at the same time? Go on a working holiday! Here are three places to try.

A Ski Resort

For anyone who loves the snow, helping out at a ski resort
5　is hardly what you would call work. Most workers ski as part of their job and can usually go skiing on the resort's slopes during their free time. Of course, that's why there is so much competition for these jobs. There are many things you could do, like being a ski instructor, a ski lift operator, or a groundskeeper.[1]
10　You can also work inside the hotels. The work is fun, but the pay is usually quite low. However, for anyone who loves the outdoors and skiing, such an opportunity is not to be missed!

A Fruit Farm

If you don't mind getting a little dirty, a farm job is an excellent choice for a working holiday in spring or autumn. The job usually　15 involves helping farmers pick fruit and plant seeds. You might also help make jams and baked goods with the fruits you pick and even get to sell your creations at local farmer's markets. While the pay isn't much, farms usually give workers food and a comfortable place to sleep for free. The best part about such　20 work is that farms are found all over the world, from New Zealand, to India, to Ecuador.

On a Yacht or Cruise Ship

Want to get paid to see the world? Find a job on a tourist yacht or a cruise ship!
25　You'll get to visit exotic places and even some hard-to-reach islands. There are many kinds of jobs available, from cooking and cleaning to organizing fun activities for the guests. Working on a ship can be stressful because there are so many things to do, and you have to take care of many people. You should be able to work well in a team and under pressure. During the warmer seasons,
30　you can stay cool in places like Alaska. When it turns cold, you can stay warm by visiting the Caribbean. It's not the most highly-paid job, but it's surely the most exciting!

---

[1]A **groundskeeper** is the person who takes care of a park or sports ground.

384 words　　**Time taken** _____

Reading Comprehension

Choose the correct answers for the following questions.

1 Where can you find work all year round?
   a on a ski resort
   b on a fruit farm
   c on a cruise ship
   d none of the above

2 In line 5, why is helping out at a ski resort *hardly work*?
   a You are not paid enough.
   b You don't have to work very hard.
   c You'll enjoy it too much.
   d You'll have a lot of free time.

3 Which of these jobs will let you travel?
   a a job as a ski instructor
   b a job picking fruit at a farm
   c a job selling things at farmer's markets
   d a job taking care of guests on a cruise ship

4 In line 29, the passage says that workers on a cruise ship must be able to work *under pressure*. This means they _____.
   a can handle stressful situations
   b do not get seasick easily
   c can work for long hours
   d have many different skills

5 Which is NOT something these jobs have in common?
   a You won't earn very much.
   b You get a free place to stay.
   c You get to meet people.
   d You'll get a little dirty.

6 This article is meant for _____.
   a hotel managers
   b students
   c ski instructors
   d working adults

Turn to page 176 to record your reading fluency progress. First, find the vertical line that is closest to your reading rate. Next, how many of the six comprehension questions did you answer correctly? Find the point on the graph where your reading rate and your comprehension score meet. Mark that spot with a dot.
Which quadrant does the dot fall in? Your goal is to be a fluent reader and score in quadrant four.

Money and Budgets

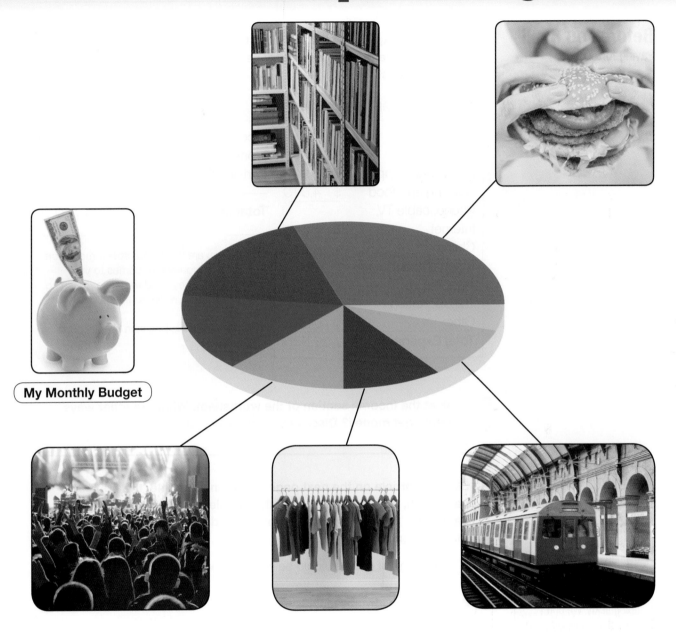

My Monthly Budget

Getting Ready

Discuss the following questions with a partner.

1 What do you spend money on? How much do you spend each month on the things in the pictures?
2 What do you wish you could spend less on?
3 What are some good ways to be careful with money?

CHAPTER 1 A Student Budget

Before You Read
Paying for College

A Look at the expenses on the Student Budget Worksheet below. How much do students in your country pay for these things? What other expenses do students have?

STUDENT BUDGET WORKSHEET (one year)

Expenses[1]		Income[2]	
Tuition[3]	$ 18,000	Money from parents	$ 20,000
Books and supplies	$ 900	Part-time[5] work	$ 5,700
Housing and food	$ 4,010		
Phone, cable TV, Internet	$ 640	**Total Income**	$ 25,700
Clothing	$ 800		
Entertainment[4] and personal	$ 1,220		
Transportation	$ 1,460		
Other	$ 500		
Total Expenses	$ 27,530		

[1] **Expenses** are things you spend money on
[2] **Income** is money that comes to you
[3] **Tuition** is money used to pay for teaching
[4] **Entertainment** refers to things you do for fun
[5] **Part-time** work is less than 35–40 hours a week.

B Look at the Income section of the worksheet. What are other ways students get money? Discuss your answers with a partner.

Reading Skill
Skimming for Main Ideas

We skim to get the main idea or ideas of the passage. When we *skim* we read over the text quickly. We don't need to read every word or look up words we do not understand. We do notice key words that are repeated.

A Skim the article on the next page. Read only the title, the first paragraph, the first sentence of the middle paragraphs, and the last paragraph. Don't worry about words you don't know. Then answer the following questions.

1 What kind of people would be interested in reading this article?
_____

2 Where would you see this article? _____

3 The main idea of this passage is _____.
   a the high cost of a university education
   b how to pay for a university education
   c living on a student budget

B Now read the entire article carefully. Then answer the questions on page 52.

A Student Budget

College is an exciting time to learn and to make friends that will last a lifetime. Many students do not like to **worry** about money, and would rather not think about it. However, it doesn't matter whether a student's parents pay for
5 everything, or whether the student works part-time to help pay for his or her **education**. All students can get into money trouble if they're not careful.

The cost of a college education can be high. In English-speaking countries, the **average** cost **per**
10 student per year can be well over US$15,000. Students must also pay for books, paper, pens, etc. These can cost $500 to $1,000 per year. Students must also pay thousands more per year for room and board.[1] Add money for clothes, travel, and other **personal**
15 expenses, and the average cost of one year at university can be $20,000 to $30,000, or more.

So, students need to spend their money carefully. At most universities, councillors[2] can give students **advice** on how to budget their money.

20 This is what they suggest: At the start of a school semester, write down your income—for example, money you will get from your family or from a part-time job. Then, **list** all of your expenses. Put your expenses into two groups: those that change (food, phone, books,
25 travel), and those that will stay the same (tuition, room and board). Add together all of your expenses. Are they more than your income? Will you need to **borrow** from family or friends, or will you need to get more money by doing part-time work? Often, students find it is easier to plan out their own budget, and save their own money, rather than trying to borrow from others.

30 As you can see, there's more to learn at college than just what's taught in the classroom!

---

[1] **Room and board** is the cost of a place to stay and eat meals.
[2] **Councillors** are people who offer helpful ideas to others.

Reading Comprehension

Check Your Understanding

A Choose the correct answers for the following questions.

1 According to the passage, what do many students think very little about?
   a studying   **b** parents   **c** money

2 Students pay about _____ for books and other things they will need in class.
   a $500 to $1,000 per year   **b** $10,000 per year   **c** $20,000 per year

3 On a list of expenses, advisors say that the cost of food and tuition should be _____ .
   a grouped together   **b** in different groups   **c** left out

4 The cost of _____ is NOT a personal expense.
   a clothes   **b** travel   **c** room and board

B Read the sentences below. Check (✓) true (T) or false (F). If the sentence is false, change it to make it true.

		T	F
1	All students can get into money trouble.		
2	Most universities have advisors who can help students to budget their money.		
3	Students must borrow money if their expenses are more than their income.		
4	Costs for clothing and travel should be part of a student's budget.		

Critical Thinking

C Discuss the following questions with a partner.

1 What are some ways that students can get into money trouble?
2 Do you think it is hard to have a part-time job while studying? Why, or why not?

Vocabulary Comprehension

Definitions

A Match each word with its definition. The words in blue are from the passage.

1 _____ per   **a** about one person, not everyone
2 _____ education   **b** to think about things you are afraid of
3 _____ list   **c** helpful ideas you get from someone
4 _____ borrow   **d** usual, normal
5 _____ worry   **e** to write down a series of items in a column
6 _____ average   **f** for each or every
7 _____ personal   **g** learning
8 _____ advice   **h** to ask someone to give you something that you will give back later

B Complete the following sentences with the correct form of the words from **A**.

1 My friend _____ $50 from me three weeks ago, but he hasn't returned the money. I'm really starting to _____ that he won't pay me back.

2 Sometimes it's easier to get a good job if you got your _____ at a good university. I went to one that was just _____. It's not the best, but isn't so bad.

3 It's important to listen to the _____ that older people give you if you want to improve.

4 Membership to the club is about $100 _____ year.

A Match each word in the box with its opposite.

| expense   inhale   exclude   import   introverted |

1 export _____

2 exhale _____

3 income _____

4 include _____

5 extroverted _____

B Write the words from **A** next to the correct definition.

1 _____ to bring things into a country

2 _____ to breathe in

3 _____ to leave out

4 _____ money that you make

5 _____ shy, quiet

C Complete the following sentences with the correct form of the words from **A**.

1 It is harmful to _____ cigarette smoke.

2 The lunches that our school serves _____ many healthy foods, such as fruits and salads.

3 Taking a vacation abroad was a very big _____. I could hardly pay for it.

4 Hailey isn't shy at all. She's quite _____, and is always talking.

5 Many supermarkets sell food that is _____ from all over the world.

Vocabulary Skill
The Prefixes *in-* and *ex-*

The prefixes *in-* (or *im-*) and *ex-* can often have opposite meanings. *In-* and *im-* often mean *inside* or *into* while *ex-* often means *out* or *away*. For example, *internal* relates to things on the inside, while *external* relates to things on the outside. Note that the *in-/im-* and *ex-* forms of the words may be different.

You can achieve great things! As you complete this unit, think about how achieving your goals here will help you achieve your overall goals for learning English.

Before You Read
Money Quiz

A   **Answer the following questions.**

  1   How often do you think about money?

     a   all the time   **b**   sometimes   **c**   never

  2   Are you careful with your money?

     a   Yes, I always keep track of how much I spend.

     b   Sometimes, it depends on how I feel.

     c   No, I usually spend when I feel like it.

  3   How often do you save money?

     a   every month   **b**   sometimes   **c**   never

  4   Do you check prices at more than one store before buying something?

     a   No, it takes too much time. I just buy what I need whatever the price.

     b   I sometimes go to other stores if the price seems high.

     c   I always check prices in more than one store.

  5   If I had $1,000, I would _____.

     a   save most of it

     b   spend some and save the rest

     c   spend it all on gifts and things I want

B   **Discuss your answers with a partner. How good are you with money?**

Reading Skill
Identifying Supporting Details

When we identify supporting details, we read carefully for the details that support a main point. Paragraphs are often organized around a main point in the first sentence, and the details that support this point follow in the paragraph. In this passage, Lisa gives details that support her answers to Young Min's questions.

A   **Scan up to line 20 of the passage on the next page. Write two details to support the idea that Lisa doesn't have much money for fun.**

  1 _____

  2 _____

B   **How can Lisa save money? Write down your ideas.**

  1 _____

  2 _____

  3 _____

  4 _____

C   **Read the last paragraph of the passage. Were your ideas in B the same as Lisa's? Discuss with a partner.**

D   **Now read the entire passage carefully. Then answer the questions on page 56.**

My Money

In this week's *Students Around the World*, Min Young Kim interviews an American university student, Lisa Conroy. They talk about living on a student budget.

Min Young: Thanks for talking with me today, Lisa. Tell us
5 a little about yourself.

Lisa: Well, I'm 21, and I'm a junior[1] at a university in Chicago.

Min Young: How are you paying for your college education?

10 **Lisa:** My expenses for every semester[2] are almost $15,000. At the start of each semester, I get $2,000 from my college scholarship. My parents pay the rest of the $10,000 tuition, and they give me $2,000 for personal expenses. I have to pay the remaining $3,000 myself.

15 **Min Young:** How do you do that?

Lisa: I have a part-time job as a waitress. I work three nights a week, and I usually **earn** about $400 a week. In a good week I can make $600, but in a bad week it can be less than $300.

Min Young: How do you spend that money?

Lisa: It helps to pay for my **rent** and meals at college. It also pays for things like my cell phone,
20 books, **transportation**, and clothes.

Min Young: You don't have much money for fun, do you?

Lisa: That's true! My mother advised me to **stick to** my budget carefully so I don't have to borrow. I don't like to **owe** money. And I don't want to pay the bank any **interest**. I hardly ever go to the movies. My roommates and I usually rent movies and **split** the cost. And, I don't go to
25 restaurants very often. My roommates and I usually cook our own food, so it's cheaper to eat.

Min Young: How else do you save money?

Lisa: I try to walk or ride my bicycle to college. Oh, and I buy a lot of my clothes at **second-hand** stores. You can find some very cheap, nice clothes in those stores. I also try to borrow books and magazines from the library, rather than buying them on my own. My roommates and I are also
30 very careful to save water and electricity, so we don't have to pay a lot for those things.

---

[1] In four-year university programs in America, a first-year student is called a *freshman*, a second-year student is called a *sophomore*, a third-year student is called a ***junior***, and a fourth-year student is called a *senior*.
[2] A **semester** is part of the school year, usually half.

Reading Comprehension
Check Your Understanding

A **Choose the correct answers for the following questions.**

1 Lisa's expenses every semester are almost _____ .
  a $2,000   b $10,000   c $15,000

2 Lisa has a part-time job at a _____ .
  a restaurant   b theater   c hotel

3 Lisa tries to stick to a budget so she doesn't have to _____ .
  a buy cheap clothes   b ride her bicycle   c borrow money

4 Which does Lisa NOT do to save money?
  a She shares food with her roommates.
  b She borrows or buys things second-hand.
  c She tries not to use too much water or electricity.

B **Read the following sentences. Check (✔) true (T) or false (F). If the sentence is false, change it to make it true.**

		T	F
1	Lisa is interviewing Min Young.		
2	Lisa's money comes from her parents.		
3	Lisa doesn't like to owe people money.		
4	Lisa usually buys clothes from second-hand stores.		

Critical Thinking

C **Discuss the following questions with a partner.**

1 What kind of person do you think Lisa is? Is she similar to you or different from you?

2 Do you buy your clothes in second-hand stores? What other things can students buy second-hand to save money?

Vocabulary Comprehension
Words in Context

A **Complete each statement with the best answer. The words in blue are from the passage.**

1 If you earn money, you _____ .
  a work for it   b receive it as a gift

2 I owe Alex some money. I have to _____ .
  a pay him back   b remind him to pay me

3 If you pay rent for something, it _____ belong to you.
  a does   b does not

Think positively! Language learners who think positive thoughts are able to stay motivated longer. Think about five things you do well as a learner when you face a challenge in this unit.

4 When you split the cost of something with a friend, _____ .

   a your friend pays   **b** you both pay

5 If you borrow $100 from the bank and must pay interest, you will return _____ in all.

   a more than $100   **b** less than $100

6 For transportation I can choose between _____ .

   a the bus or the subway   **b** the cafeteria or a restaurant

7 Melissa and Joan really stick to their budgets, so they _____ .

   a don't have much money for fun

   b can spend as much as they want

8 Which of these can you buy from a second-hand store?

   a a computer   **b** food

B **Complete the following sentences with the words in blue from A. You might have to change the form of the word.**

1 I _____ $200 a week from my part-time job.

2 It's important that I _____ my plan and not give up.

3 Most students use public _____ , such as the subway.

4 Every month, my housemates and I pay the _____ together.

5 I _____ the cost of his birthday present with a few people.

6 Many people borrow money to pay for their university education, and they often still _____ money to the bank many years later.

A **The words in the box are all used to talk about money. Some are used to talk about money coming in to you (I); others are used to talk about money going out (O). Write I or O next to the correct word.**

1 expense ___	**2** borrow ___	**3** income ___	**4** earn ___
5 buy ___	**6** lend ___	**7** owe ___	
8 rent ___	**9** pay ___	**10** spend ___	

B **Complete the sentences below with the words from A.**

1 My brother wants me to _____ him some money.

2 How much did you _____ for that T-shirt?

3 I think we have to _____ an air conditioner. The temperature hit 38 degrees Celsius today.

4 I recently got a part-time job, so my monthly _____ has gone up.

5 How much do you usually _____ each month on food?

Vocabulary Skill
Organizing Vocabulary:
Words Relating to Money

When you learn new vocabulary, it can help you to think about other words that are used to talk about the same topic. We can divide these words into groups to help us remember them better.

Real Life Skill
Creating a Personal Budget

A personal budget can help you spend your money more carefully. But most people don't create a personal budget because they think it is difficult. Actually, creating a personal budget can be quite simple and fun. With a little practice, anyone can improve their budgeting skills.

A **Create a personal monthly budget. Follow the steps below.**

Step 1: Write your income for one month.

Monthly Income:	$1,500

Step 2: Write down all the expenses that you have each month. Think about how much you spend each month on them. Write down how much you spend on each and add the numbers.

Rent	$800
Food	$200
Transport	$100
Heat & Electricity	$50
Necessary Expenses	$1,150

Step 3: Now write down how much you spend on other things. Add the numbers.

Restaurants	$150
Movies	$60
Music CDs	$100
Other Expenses	$310

Step 4: Add all your expenses together and subtract them from your income. Then you'll see how much extra money you have every month.

Income	$1,500
Expenses	$1,460
Extra Money!	$40

B **Internet Challenge: Use the search words *student*, *budget*, and *worksheet* to find student budget worksheets online. Use your dictionary to look up words you don't know. Print out or copy the worksheet and share it with a group of classmates.**

What do you think?

1 What are some ways that parents can teach their children to spend money carefully?
2 What are some popular ways for students to make extra money?
3 If you have extra money at the end of the month, what would you do with it?

Our Modern Lifestyle

Cell Phones

	Agree	Disagree
1 It makes me angry when people talk loudly on their cell phones in public places.	☐	☐
2 People shouldn't drive and talk on a cell phone at the same time. It's really dangerous.	☐	☐
3 I'm afraid I'll lose my cell phone with all my information inside.	☐	☐
4 People shouldn't use their cell phones at the dining table. I think it's very rude.	☐	☐

5 Your idea: _____

_____

The Internet

	Agree	Disagree
1 People shouldn't try to get music from the Internet without paying for it.	☐	☐
2 I don't buy things on the Internet because I'm afraid people will steal my information.	☐	☐
3 It worries me that people are watching me when I email or use the Internet.	☐	☐
4 People shouldn't put other people's information or pictures online without asking them first.	☐	☐

5 Your idea: _____

_____

Getting Ready

A Think about answers to the following questions.

1 Look at the technology concerns above. Check (✓) whether you agree or disagree with each one.

2 Write one more concern about cell phones and one about the Internet.

B Discuss your answers with a partner. Do you have the same kind of concerns?

CHAPTER 1 Cell Phone Etiquette

Before You Read
Using Cell Phones

A Think about answers to the following questions.

1 Is it okay to use a cell phone in these places? Why, or why not?

2 *Etiquette* refers to a set of rules for polite behavior, which can be official or unofficial. What do you think the rules of etiquette should be for using cell phones in a classroom?

B Discuss your answers with a partner.

Reading Skill
Identifying Transition Words

> It is very important to know about transition words and how they show the relationship between ideas. A good understanding of transition words can improve your understanding and reading speed.

A Scan the letter on the next page to find the transition words or phrases in the box. (Circle) them in the letter.

likewise	in fact	additionally	that's why
furthermore	for instance	on the other hand	

B Write the transition word or phrase next to their use. Some may have more than one use.

1 to show a result _that's why_

2 to give more information _____

3 to show that something is the same _____

4 to show that something is different _____

5 to give examples _____

C Read the entire letter carefully. Then answer the questions on page 62.

Cell Phone Etiquette

Dear *Sunday Globe*,

I am writing to you about your article in last Sunday's newspaper, "Cell Phones Make Life Easier." You did an excellent job explaining the good points of cell phones: they're **convenient**, we feel safer always being able to call someone, and they are very helpful in business. On the other hand, you didn't talk about their bad points at all. I hope you'll let me give your readers some advice on cell phone etiquette.

The first point I'd like to **address** is when not to use your phone. It's polite to switch off your phone or turn off the sound when you're in class or in a meeting. If you get an important call, you should ask for permission to leave the room and then don't talk for too long. Furthermore, for conversations that need more time, it is best to ask the person to call back at a more convenient time. Cell phones can also cause you to neglect[1] the people you are with. I find it really **annoying** when my friends **constantly** check their messages on their phone. In fact, I want to tell them to turn off the cell phone and enjoy my company!

Another point that needs to be made has to do with personal space. I think it is very **impolite** to make calls in small spaces or crowded rooms. This makes others uncomfortable and forces them to listen to your personal conversations. Additionally, it disturbs other face-to-face conversations; that's why I never use my cell phone within a few meters of other people except in **emergencies**.

Lastly, I would like readers to **pay attention** to the dangers of using your phone while doing something else. For instance, driving and texting is a bad **combination**. Likewise, using your phone or texting when walking can make you careless. You don't want to get hit by a car. Pay attention to where you're going!

Sincerely,
Amber Jala

---

[1] When you **neglect** someone or something, you don't notice or take care of them.

Reading Comprehension
Check Your Understanding

A **Choose the correct answers for the following questions.**

1 Why did Amber decide to write this letter?
   a She wanted to talk about the good points of cell phones.
   b She thought the bad points of cell phones weren't included in the article.
   c She thought the *Sunday Globe* should not be writing about cell phones.

2 According to Amber, it is polite to _____ when taking a phone call.
   a speak quietly
   b speak slowly and clearly
   c move away from other people

3 According to Amber, you should only answer you phone when _____.
   a it's an emergency
   b you're having lunch with a friend
   c you're in a crowded room

4 Amber thinks that if you talk on your cell phone while doing something else, you _____.
   a will save a lot of time
   b will enjoy yourself more
   c might not pay attention to what you're doing

B **Write the number of the paragraph (1–4) that best matches each statement.**

   a _____ Never make a call in a car full of people.
   b _____ If the call is going to be long, do it at another time.
   c _____ Don't talk on your phone and pay for something at the same time.
   d _____ Turn off your phone.

Critical Thinking

C **Discuss the following questions with a partner.**

1 Do you agree with the rules in the letter? Which of them do you follow?
2 Think of other examples of why cell phones makes things more convenient.

Vocabulary Comprehension
Odd Word Out

A **For each group, circle the word that does not belong. The words in blue are from the passage.**

1	address	speak to	listen
2	notice	pay attention	neglect
3	mix	company	combination
4	convenient	awesome	excellent
5	problem	emergency	joke
6	rarely	always	constantly
7	impolite	kind	nice
8	annoying	upsetting	loud

B Complete the following sentences using words in blue from A.

1 I've reported the problem many times, but no one has tried to
   _____ it.
2 Kim must be very popular. Her phone is _____ ringing.
3 Please _____. I have some very important news.
4 For me, the subway is the most _____ form of transportation.
   Trains come every ten minutes during the day.

A Look at this chart of different relationships between ideas, and the
transition words that show the relationships.

Relationship	Transition words
show a result	thus; therefore; that's why
give more information	in addition; additionally; furthermore; in fact
compare	likewise; similarly
contrast	in contrast; on the other hand; however
give examples	for example; for instance

Vocabulary Skill
Using Transition Words

Transition words show the relationship between ideas. Knowing them and their uses makes reading much easier. They can also help you to write more interesting sentences.

B Complete the following sentences with the transition words from A.
There may be more than one correct answer for each question.

1 That country has many unusual customs; _____, when people
   meet someone, they hit the person on the head.
2 I was so embarrassed that my picture appeared in the newspaper
   without my permission; _____ I have written a letter to the
   newspaper asking them to apologize.
3 I always write in my travel journal when I am on vacation;
   _____, my sister has a notebook in which she writes down
   everything we do on vacation.
4 I spend all the money I earn very quickly and never save any;
   _____, my brother sticks to a budget and saves a lot of money
   every month.
5 I've borrowed more money than I can pay back. I owe $100 to Sergio,
   $50 to Simon, $75 to Ryoko, and $500 for the rent; _____,
   I owe $700 in income taxes this year!
6 I've been wearing second-hand clothes all my life, and I'm tired of it.
   _____ I'm going shopping for new clothes this weekend!
7 I'm naturally a curious person; _____, my mother is always
   asking questions and wants to know everything.

> **Learning English is valuable!** You can have meaningful experiences that will provide satisfaction
> and enrich your life. On a piece of paper, list five ways that you believe learning English will enrich your life.

CHAPTER 2 Smartphone Apps for Travelers

Before You Read
Applications

A Think about answers to the following questions.

1 Do you use apps on your phone? If so, which ones?
2 Look at this list of different kinds of apps. Circle the apps you would be interested in using.

cooking	business	planning	_____
games	photos	travel	_____
sports	movies	foreign language	_____

B Discuss your answers with a partner. Together, think of three more kinds of apps to complete the box.

Reading Skill
Making Inferences

When we make inferences, we look at the information that the writer states directly and use it to make guesses about information that the writer has left out. Making inferences is important because sometimes the writer doesn't tell us everything. By making inferences we can be active readers and understand more.

A Scan the passage on the next page to find the words in bold below. Read the content around the words and make inferences about the meanings. Circle the best answer to complete each statement.

1 In line 10, **translates** probably means _____.
   a changes the language
   b speaks to you
   c plays music
2 In line 14, **frequent** probably means _____.
   a rare   b never   c often
3 In line 18, **combines** probably means _____.
   a takes apart   b puts together   c moves away from
4 What is an example of **travel confirmation documents**, mentioned in line 19?
   a homework
   b airline reservation email
   c a travel journal
5 Which sentence below has the same meaning as *a guidebook typically helps you only in places the average tourist goes*?
   a A guidebook *usually* helps you only in places the average tourist goes.
   b A guidebook *never* helps you in places the average tourist goes.
   c A guidebook *always* helps you in places the average tourist goes.

B Read the entire article carefully. Then answer the questions on page 66.

Smartphone Apps for Travelers

Traveling soon? Smartphone apps make traveling easier than ever. Unfortunately, with thousands of new travel-related apps to choose from each month, it can take a long time to figure out which applications are truly helpful. Here are three apps that will definitely make your next trip abroad a little easier.

Talk to Me

5

Say au revoir[1] to language phrase books[2] after **downloading** the Talk to Me smartphone app. This is a great tool for anyone visiting a foreign country—**it** works like a translator in your pocket! When you speak into the phone in English, it **translates** what you are saying into the language you select. You can choose between English, Chinese, French, Spanish, German, and Italian. This app is useful for the everyday needs of tourists and business travelers. It's also great for **frequent** travelers and language learners.

10

15

Tripit

Are you always looking for your travel information when it's time to check in for your flight? Tripit **combines** all of your travel **confirmation** documents, such as hotel room bookings, into one travel itinerary. Users send their travel-related emails to Tripit, and the app turns it into an easy-to-use itinerary with a calendar. Tripit also **prepares** maps and weather information for the places on your itinerary.

20

CitySeekr

25

Imagine being able to find whatever you need, no matter where you are! A map easily becomes outdated, and a guidebook **typically** helps you only in places the average tourist goes. What you need on your trip is an app that will tell you where the **locals** go. Want to find a great sushi place in Singapore? Morning coffee in Barcelona? A tailor in Mexico City? The CitySeekr app helps you find these places. It uses information created by Singaporeans, Spanish, Mexicans, and people from other popular tourist cities, to give advice on restaurants, gas stations, shops, landmarks, and more.

30

35

---

[1] Say **au revoir** when you want to say "goodbye" in French.
[2] A **phrase book** is a book to help travelers speak another language.

Reading Comprehension
Check Your Understanding

A **Choose the correct answers for the following questions.**

1 Why can it take a long time to find a good travel app?
   a There are so many to choose from.
   b Many of them are hard to use.
   c They are only available for one month.

2 Why does the author tell readers to say au revoir *to language phrase books* (line 6) after getting Talk to Me?
   a Talk to Me is much better than language phrase books.
   b Language phrase books will no longer be printed.
   c Talk to Me will teach you the meaning of *au revoir*.

3 What does **it** refer to in line 8?
   a the smartphone   b a foreign land   c Talk to Me

4 **Locals** (line 30) refers to people who _____.
   a live and work in the area
   b create maps and guidebooks
   c created the CitySeekr app

B **Read the following sentences. Check (✓) the app(s) that best match(es) each sentence. You may check more than one app.**

This app is for people who …	Talk to Me	Tripit	CitySeekr
1 are visiting a country for the first time			
2 want to find cool shops and restaurants			
3 want to order a meal in another language			
4 want all their travel information in one place			
5 are going on a short business trip			

Critical Thinking

C **Discuss the following questions with a partner.**

1 Would you use a travel app instead of a guidebook? Why, or why not?
2 How else has technology changed how we travel?

Vocabulary Comprehension
Definitions

A **Match each word with its definition. The words in blue are from the passage.**

1 _____ download   a to put together or make
2 _____ translate   b to change into a different language
3 _____ frequent   c to blend; to mix together
4 _____ confirmation   d to get a file from the Internet
5 _____ combine   e to think about something that isn't real
6 _____ typically   f making sure of something
7 _____ prepare   g often
8 _____ imagine   h normally

B **Answer the following questions, then discuss your answers with a partner. The words in blue are from the passage.**

1 Describe a typical day in your life.
2 What skills do you think a translator needs?
3 Do you download things over the Internet? Give some examples.
4 What would you prepare before you go on a trip?

A **Create a word web about apps. Use words in the box and other words from this chapter. Explain your diagram to a partner.**

~~apps~~	frequent	locals	guidebooks
documents	calendar	combines	itinerary
~~translate~~	food	language	easy-to-use
confirmation	prepare	information	

Vocabulary Skill
Word Webs

A helpful way to remember new vocabulary is to create a *word web*. Word webs can help you to link the new words you have learned to vocabulary you already know. It can also be used to identify the main ideas in the passage and help you create a summary.

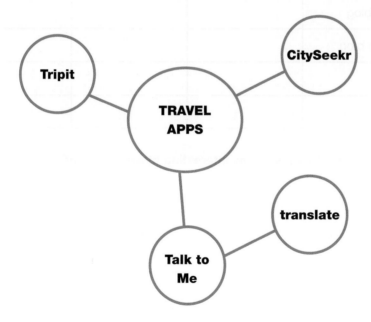

B **Now try making a word web using words you found in another chapter. See how many branches and words you can add. Share your ideas with a partner.**

Monitor your improvements. When you have finished the unit, identify two things that you did well during this unit. As a class, talk about the improvements that you are making as readers. Make a list and post it on the wall in the classroom. Review the list regularly over the next week.

Real Life Skill

Reading Blogs

A blog is a kind of website. There are many different types of blogs with lots of different information, but in some ways blogs are also much the same. They all have posts. Posts are like short passages on a blog. Posts nearly always have a date and a title. Remember, in a typical blog, the newest post is on top.

A **Using a computer, follow these steps to collect some information about a blog.**

1 Search the Internet using the search words *travel blog*.
2 Click on one of the travel blogs you found.
  a What is the name of the blog? _____
  b What is the title of the newest post? _____
  c What is the date of the newest post? _____

B **Now do four more Internet searches to complete the chart. Then do two more searches using your own Internet search words.**

Internet search words	The name of the blog	The title of the newest post	The date of the newest post
soccer blog			
movie blog			
music blog			
English blog			

C **Tell your partner about any interesting blogs you found.**

What do you think?

1 Do you think that new technologies make our lives better? If so, in what ways?
2 Some people say there is too much information in the world today. Do you agree or disagree? Explain your answer.
3 Do you have a personal webpage or blog? If so, describe it.

Getting Ready

Discuss the following questions with a partner.

1 Do you know the names of these Olympic events? What other Olympic events can you name?

2 What are the names of some cities where the Olympic Games have been held?

3 Have you watched the Olympics before? Which events do you like?

CHAPTER 1 The Olympic Flame

Before You Read
An Olympic Flame Quiz

A Read the sentences below. Check (✓) true (T) or false (F).

		T	F
1	The flame is a symbol of the spirit of the Olympics.		
2	Only athletes can carry the torch.		
3	The torch relay is a modern addition to the Olympics.		
4	The torch relay happens only during the Summer Olympic Games.		
5	The torch design has remained the same since it started.		
6	It is the flame, not the torch, that is passed from person to person.		

B Discuss your answers in **A** with a partner. Then check your answers at the bottom on the next page.

Reading Skill
Skimming for the Main Idea

> Skimming means reading quickly to get a general idea of what a passage is about. When we skim we don't need to read every word or look up words we don't understand. We just need to understand the main ideas of a passage.

A Skim the passage on the next page. Read only the first line of each paragraph. Then answer the following question.

This passage is mainly about _____ .

a the sports in the Summer Olympic Games
b the tradition of the Olympic flame and torch relay
c the Olympics in ancient Greece

B Now skim paragraphs 2, 3, and 4. (Circle) the main idea for each one.

Paragraph 2
a The flame must be created using sunlight and a mirror.
b The torch relay is an ancient Olympic tradition.

Paragraph 3
a Carrying the torch is a very special honor.
b People with disabilities can carry the torch.

Paragraph 4
a The torch is usually carried on foot.
b The torch can be carried in many different ways.

C Read the entire passage carefully. Then answer the questions on page 72.

Monitor your motivation. Your motivation level can be high, medium, or low. During this chapter, stop four times and monitor your level. If it is low, what can you do to increase it? As a class, talk about what you can do to keep your motivation high.

The Olympic Flame

1 Every four years, the Summer Olympic Games **kick off** with an elaborate[1] opening ceremony that welcomes athletes from every competing nation. However, preparations and celebrations for the Olympic Games start long before the opening ceremony.
5 The true beginning of the Olympic celebration is the **lighting** of the Olympic torch and the relay that carries the flame to the host city.

2 The Olympic torch is lit at a ceremony in Olympia, Greece, where the ancient[2] games were held. One **requirement** for the Olympic flame is that it must be created using only sunlight and a mirror. The flame is lit months before the games, and the first
10 runner begins the great relay among the ruins[3] of an ancient Olympic stadium.

3 The first modern Olympic torch relay **took place** in Berlin, in the summer of 1936. At the beginning, runners were mainly **selected** from the Olympic athletes, but later regular citizens—including children, old people, and people with disabilities—began to participate as well. Carrying the torch
15 is a once-in-a-lifetime opportunity and a great **honor**.

4 Traditionally, the torch is carried **on foot**. However, sometimes other kinds of transport are needed. When the torch must go
20 overseas, it is sent on a private plane. The torch has also been carried underwater. For the Sydney Summer Games in 2000, a diver swam with the torch!

5 At the end of the relay, the flame is used to light a giant pot. The light, a **symbol** of
25 the Olympic spirit, burns throughout the games.

---

[1] Something that is **elaborate** is complex and has a lot of different parts.
[2] Something that is **ancient** is very, very old.
[3] **Ruins** are the remains of a very old building.

Olympic Flame Quiz answers: 1. T; 2. F; 3. F; 4. F; 5. F; 6. T

Reading Comprehension

Check Your Understanding

A **Choose the correct answers for the following questions.**

1 The Olympic Games truly begin when _____.
  a the opening ceremony takes place
  b the Olympic torch is lit
  c athletes from competing nations arrive

2 The torch is lit in Greece because that is where the _____.
  a ancient games were held
  b Olympics are held every year
  c flame is always burning

3 At first, _____ were selected to carry the torch.
  a athletes   b children   c citizens

4 When the torch reaches the host city, the Olympic flame _____.
  a is put out   b lights a big pot   c is carried underwater

B **Read the sentences below. Check (✓) true (T) or false (F). If the sentence is false, change it to make it true.**

		T	F
1	The first modern Olympic torch relay took place in the summer of 2000 for the Sydney Games.		
2	The torch is always carried on foot.		
3	The Olympic flame is created using sunlight and a mirror.		
4	The light continues to burn during the games.		
5	The Olympic flame is a very important part of the Olympic Games.		

Critical Thinking

C **Discuss the following questions with a partner.**

1 Why is the Olympic flame created using only sunlight and a mirror?
2 Do you think the flame is a good symbol of the Olympic spirit? Why, or why not?

Vocabulary Comprehension

Words in Context

A **Complete each statement with the best answer. The words in blue are from the passage.**

1 A _____ is used to symbolize a country's beliefs and goals.
  a flag   b map

2 Since you're going there on foot, you should carry _____ with you.
  a less   b more

3 Which of these can be considered an honor?
  a working on a class project
  b representing your school in a competition

4 Which of these can take place?

    a an item   **b** an event

5 He had to light a candle because the room was so _____.

    a bright   **b** dark

6 One requirement of learning at school is to _____.

    a do homework   **b** get a job

7 To select a university means to _____ a school.

    a leave   **b** choose

8 Tina kicked off the party by _____.

    a saying goodbye to everyone   **b** welcoming everyone

B **Answer the following questions, then discuss your answers with a partner. The words in blue are from the passage.**

1 What is used in your country to symbolize your culture?

2 Where do you usually go on foot?

3 What are the requirements for you to get a job?

4 What do universities want to know when they select new students?

A **Write the noun form of each of these verbs. Only four of them use the suffix -ment. Use your dictionary to help you.**

1	agree	_____	**5**	judge _____
2	argue	_____	**6**	refuse _____
3	arrange	_____	**7**	select _____
4	imagine	_____	**8**	submit _____

B **Add the suffix -ment to the verbs in the box to form nouns. Use the nouns to complete the sentences below.**

> announce   achieve   encourage   require
>
> entertain   govern   improve

1 Did you hear that _____ about the meeting tomorrow?

2 The _____ of the United States is located in Washington, D.C.

3 I was really nervous about speaking in front of the class, but my teacher's words of _____ made me feel much better.

4 His English skills have been showing _____ since he started reading more.

5 It was a huge _____ for him to walk on his own after he hurt his legs in the accident.

6 One _____ of this course is a final exam.

7 The company paid a magician to provide _____ at the office party.

Vocabulary Skill
The Suffix -ment

> One of the uses of the suffix -ment is to change certain verbs into nouns. For example, when we add the suffix -ment to the verb embarrass, the verb becomes the noun embarrassment.

CHAPTER 2 Unusual Olympic Sports

Before You Read
Unusual Sports

A Answer the following questions.

1 Look at this list of Olympic events. (Circle) the ones that you know.

> archery   canoeing   fencing   synchronised-
>
> snowboarding   taekwondo   water polo   swimming
>
> bobsledding   tug-of-war

2 One of the events in **A** used to be an Olympic event, but it isn't anymore. Which one do you think it is?

3 Now look at the pictures of three unusual Olympic sports on the next page. Do you think that these are unusual sports? Why, or why not?

B Discuss your answers with a partner.

Reading Skill
Reading for Details

> Reading for details is a two-step process. First, scan to find the part of the passage that has the information you want. Second, read every word in the sentence and make sure you understand the meaning. This can be useful when taking tests.

A Read each of the following sections in the passage on the next page. Check (✓) true (T), false (F), or not given (NG). If the sentence is false, change it to make it true.

Curling	T	F	NG
1 Curling is played on ice.			
2 There are six players on each team.			
3 The stones never touch the center of the house.			

Trampoline	T	F	NG
4 Trampoline is a gymnastic sport.			
5 Judges look at how many tricks a gymnast can do.			
6 America had only one trampoline gymnast in the 2000 Olympics.			

Skeleton	T	F	NG
7 Early skeleton sleds were made out of bones.			
8 The 1980 Winter Olympics were held in New York.			
9 Zach Gale competed in the 1980 Winter Olympics.			

B Read the entire passage carefully. Then answer the questions on page 76.

www.olympiccareers.heinle.com/athletes

Unusual Olympic Sports

For many people, the Olympic Games consist of popular sports like swimming, running, or ice skating. Here are three unusual Olympic events, and three athletes who fell in love with them.

Curling •

Curling is a sport that is played on ice. Two teams of four
5   players each **slide** eight stones along the ice to a colored
circle (called the *house*). The **object** of the game is to
place a stone closest to the center of the house.

"I started curling very young," Canadian Olympic curler
Sammy McCann told us. "My father **managed** a hotel with
10 an ice rink. As soon as the people left the ice, my friends
and I would get right on and start curling."

•*Trampoline*

Kids have been jumping on trampolines for almost a hundred years,
but it was only at the 2000 Olympic Games in Sydney that trampoline
became an official Olympic sport. In Olympic competitions, each   15
trampoline gymnast is **judged** on ten different skills. A gymnast
can score well by showing that they can **control** their bodies while
jumping high and twisting and flipping smoothly in the air.

"I love the sport. I've been doing it since I was five years old,"
said Jennifer Parilla, American trampoline gymnast. After Jennifer   20
competed in the 2000 Olympics (as the only American trampoline
gymnast), she got a tattoo of a butterfly to remind her of her "new
beginnings" as an Olympian.

Skeleton •

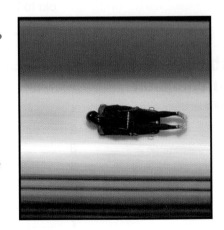

25 The sport of skeleton racing first became an Olympic sport
in 1928. Skeleton **racers** slide down an icy course at very
high speed on a simple sled. The sled is called a skeleton
because early sleds **looked like** human skeletons.

"I didn't start skeleton until I was 30," said American
30 skeleton racer Zach Gale. "While driving, my girlfriend and I
took a wrong turn at Lake Placid, New York; that's where
the 1980 Winter Olympics took place. They were offering
skeleton classes that afternoon. My girlfriend said, 'Why
don't we give it a try?' It was fun! I fell in love with it."

Reading Comprehension
Check Your Understanding

A Choose the correct answers for the following questions.

1 This passage is about _____ .
   a how to become an Olympic athlete
   b how Olympic athletes first started in their sports
   c why curling, trampoline, and skeleton are Olympic events

2 Jennifer Parilla got a tattoo to remind her of her first _____ .
   a trampoline   b butterfly   c Olympics

3 These athletes took up the sport because _____ .
   a they fell in love with it
   b their parents told them to do it
   c they wanted to enter the Olympics

4 Which athlete became interested in the sport later in life?
   a Sammy McCann   b Jennifer Parilla   c Zach Gale

B Read the following sentences. Check (✓) the sport(s) that best match(es) each sentence. You may check more than one sport.

This sport ...	Curling	Trampoline	Skeleton
1 is held on ice.			
2 has judges to look at different skills.			
3 has two teams that compete against each other.			
4 is named after the main object the athletes use.			
5 involves going at very high speeds.			

Critical Thinking

C Discuss the following questions with a partner.

1 Why do some people prefer these sports to more popular ones?
2 At what age do Olympic athletes usually begin training? How old is too old to be an Olympic athlete?

Vocabulary Comprehension
Definitions

A Match each word with its definition. The words in blue are from the passage.

1 _____ control   a to seem the same
2 _____ look like   b to take care of (a business)
3 _____ object   c move over a smooth surface
4 _____ race   d a speed competition (in running)
5 _____ slide   e goal; the main idea of a game
6 _____ take a wrong turn f to decide who is the winner
7 _____ judge   g to go left instead of right, or right instead of left
8 _____ manage   h to make something or someone do what you want

B **Complete the following sentences using the words in blue from A. You might have to change the form of the word.**

1 Athletes usually have excellent _____ over their bodies.
2 When the _____ began, the competitors jumped on their sleds and began to _____ down the slope.
3 It's hard to _____ who is the better player. They're both equally good!
4 On my first day of school, I was late for class because I _____ and went to the wrong classroom.

A **Put these sports words into one of the categories below. Can you add other words? Discuss your answers with a partner.**

court	racket	player	ice rink	champion
ball	competitor	opponent	puck	sticks
stadium	skates	coach	field	gloves
sled	course	team	ring	manager

Vocabulary Skill
Organizing Vocabulary:
Words Relating to Sports

One helpful way to remember new words is to put them into meaningful groups or categories—for example, positive and negative, or people, places, and things. Putting vocabulary in groups like this can help you to remember new words and relate them to other words you know.

Sports places	Sports equipment	Sports people
court	racket	player

B **Now complete the following sentences using the correct form of words from A.**

1 There are four _____ on a curling _____.
2 Football is usually played on a(n) _____.
3 You play tennis on a(n) _____ with a(n) _____ and a _____.
4 Boxers wear big _____ and fight in a(n) _____.
5 Ice dancing competitions usually take place on a(n) _____, and the competitors wear _____.
6 Field hockey and ice hockey are played with _____. In ice hockey there is no ball; instead players use a(n) _____.

Real Life Skill

Understanding
Punctuation

> Punctuation marks—
> small symbols like
> , ! ? —are important
> because they help
> show the meaning of
> the sentence and how
> it should be read. To
> read and write English
> well you need to
> understand how, why,
> and when punctuation
> marks are used.

A **Find one example of each punctuation mark below in the passage on page 75 and (circle) it. Then write the letter of each description next to the correct punctuation mark.**

1	_____	.	period	**a**	shows what a person said
2	_____	,	comma	**b**	shows the end of a strong or surprising sentence
3	_____	;	semi-colon	**c**	shows the end of a question
4	_____	:	colon	**d**	shows the end of a sentence
5	_____	( )	parentheses	**e**	separates words or parts of a sentence
6	_____	?	question mark	**f**	separates a sentence, usually before a list
7	_____	!	exclamation point	**g**	shows a separate idea inside a sentence
8	_____	" "	quotation marks	**h**	shows that two ideas go together

B **Now add punctuation marks to these sentences. Compare your answers with a partner's.**

1 After the host city was selected work began on the new sports center
2 My father said I am not angry with you
3 I have applied for a job at three companies Acer Motorola and Westinghouse
4 She refused to address the problem she said she didn't have the time
5 Call the police This is an emergency
6 She kept asking me Are you angry
7 I like soccer and basketball but I really don't like baseball
8 For dinner last night we had take-out from a Vietnamese restaurant

> **Read for pleasure, not just for class.** Make reading fun, and it will become easier.
> Read a popular magazine or book, and you'll have interesting things to say to your classmates and to your English-speaking friends.

What do you think?

1 Can you think of sports that aren't in the Olympic Games now, but could be in the future?
2 Do you think the Olympic Games are becoming more popular or less popular?
3 Which countries do well at the Olympic Games? Why do you think so?

Fluency Strategy: KWL

Readers can ask themselves three questions to improve their reading fluency and comprehension. The letters **K**, **W**, and **L** can be used to remind you of these questions. **KWL** stands for **K**now, **W**ant, and **L**earn.

Know

The first step in the **KWL** sequence is similar to the **Survey** step in **SQ3R** (page 41) and the **A** in the **ACTIVE** approach (inside front cover). This step will help you prepare yourself before you begin reading.

A Look at the title on the right, taken from the passage on the next page. Note that a scholarship refers to an amount of money given to a (good) student to pay for their education. Now, from just the title, answer the question: *What is the topic of the passage?*

Not Your Regular Scholarship

B Ask yourself: *What do I already know about this topic?* Write down three or four things that you already know about the topic in the *Know* column of the chart below.

Know	Want	Learn

Want

In the second stage of **KWL**, ask yourself: *What do I **want** to learn as I read?* When you are reading to find out something specific, you are reading with purpose. This step is similar to the **Question** step in **SQ3R**.

A Read the passage on the next page. As you read, ask yourself: *What do I want to learn?* Write down three or four things you hope to learn in the *Want* column above.

Not Your Regular Scholarship

Life as a student can be very expensive. The cost of university tuition is increasing every year, and with all the studying students have to do, there isn't much time left for earning money. Fortunately, there are thousands of scholarships available to help students pay their bills. Scholarships are normally given to students based on how good their grades are, or how well
5   they do in sports. However, there *are* scholarship programs that choose their scholars based on factors other than grades or athletic ability. Here are some non-traditional[1] scholarships that are helping students pay their way through school.

The Tall Clubs International Scholarship

Students who are under 21 years of age and about to start university for the first time can receive up to $1,000 from Tall   10 Clubs International. This club was started to help tall people get to know each other and share what is great about height. To get this scholarship, you must be very, well, tall! Women must be at least 5'10" (177.5 centimeters) and men must be at least 6'2" (188 centimeters) to qualify.   15

The *Excellence in Predicting the Future* Award

Adventures in Education, a student loan company, awards this bimonthly[2] scholarship to encourage students to study Economics in college. Interested students can register online and use fake money to "buy" and "sell" predictions about the future,   20 in the same way that he or she might buy and sell stock[3] on the stock market. At the end of each two-month period, the students who have made the most money are given some money to help pay for college.

The Duck Tape *Stuck at Prom* Award

25   Wearing a suit and dress made out of sticky tape might not be so fashionable, but at least it pays! High school couples who attend prom in clothes made using Duck Brand sticky tape may win *Stuck at Prom* scholarships that range from $500 to $5,000. Students must create original outfits and take a photo to be shown on the company website. People will then vote on the best outfit. There is a lot of competition for this scholarship, and recent winners have
30   created extremely creative outfits.

---

[1] Something that is **traditional** has happened for a long time and is seen as normal.
[2] Something that happens **bimonthly** happens once every two months.
[3] To buy **stock** is to buy small parts of a company.

Learn

Now that you have finished reading, ask yourself: *What did I **learn** while reading?* Did you learn what you wanted to? This step is similar to the **Review** and **Recite** stages of **SQ3R** (page 43).

A Write down three or four things you learned from the passage in the Learn column of the chart on page 79.

B Choose the correct answers for the following questions.

1 The main idea of this reading is to _____ .
   a   explain why students often don't have enough money
   b   inform students about non-traditional scholarships
   c   show the difference between traditional and non-traditional scholarships
   d   encourage students not to borrow money

2 Who will probably NOT win a traditional scholarship?
   a   someone who represents the school in tennis
   b   someone in the advanced science class
   c   someone who has a business outside of school
   d   someone who gets top marks for exams

3 According to the passage, why might students not have enough time to earn money?
   a   They are busy playing sports.
   b   They have a lot of studying to do.
   c   They have to make predictions of real-world events.
   d   They are competing for scholarships.

4 Which scholarship challenges students to be creative?
   a   Tall Clubs International's scholarship
   b   Excellence in Predicting the Future
   c   Stuck at Prom
   d   none of the above

5 Which scholarship is awarded for something students have no control over?
   a   Tall Clubs International's scholarship
   b   Excellence in Predicting the Future
   c   Stuck at Prom
   d   all of them

6 Which scholarship is for students who are good at math?
   a   Tall Clubs International's scholarship
   b   Excellence in Predicting the Future
   c   Stuck at Prom
   d   none of them

SELF CHECK

Answer the following questions.

1 Have you ever used the **KWL** method before?

☐ Yes   ☐ No   ☐ I'm not sure.

2 Do you think **KWL** is helpful? Why, or why not?

_____

_____

3 How can you practice **KWL** in your reading outside of English class?

_____

_____

4 When you are reading, do you find yourself having to translate? If so, what can you do to break the habit?

_____

_____

5 Which of the six reading passages in units 4–6 did you enjoy most? Why?

_____

_____

6 Which of the six reading passages in units 4–6 was easiest? Which was most difficult? Why?

_____

_____

7 What improvements are you making as a reader? Look again at the *Tips for Fluent Reading* on pages 8 and 9. Write down one or two things that you know you can do better today than when you started this course.

_____

_____

8 What other improvements do you want to make as a reader?

_____

_____

Fluency Practice

Time yourself as you read through the passage. Write your time in the space at the bottom of the page. Then answer the questions on the next page.

Real Mail vs. Email

Meredith: "I keep it real."

Thomas: "I'll send you an email."

Sure, sending an email is fast and convenient, and there are times when it's necessary, but I think it's too impersonal. I think email makes communication less meaningful because people usually only glance[1] at their emails. They give more attention to real letters.

I think sending a real letter shows that you care about the person. It takes time to prepare, which shows that the writer is being more thoughtful than when he or she quickly types an email. Getting a handwritten note makes the person feel special. I love finding handwritten letters in my mailbox.

I also write letters because I like to make art. I make my own envelopes and write notes on colorful magazine pages. It makes my letters more interesting, and it lets me reuse, and save, paper. When I send a real letter that I made myself, I imagine the other person really enjoying it. My friends understand that I made it just for them, and I'm sending them more than just words on a page.

My life changed after I bought my first smartphone. I hardly ever pick up a pen these days because I use my phone for everything—planning my schedule, reading the news, or writing emails.

I also use email a lot. My friends all moved away to different places after high school, and I don't have time to sit down and write and post letters to them every week. Sending them emails is so much more convenient. With email, I can write to them whenever I want. Then, they can read my emails right away and send a reply just as fast.

With emails, I can reach many people at the same time. When I want to say "hi!" to old friends, I just put in their email addresses, type up a note, and send it out—no paper, no stamps, no waiting for the letters to travel over land and sea. Email helps people keep in touch, and, in the end, that's what's important, right?

[1] When you **glance** at something, you look at it quickly before looking away.

364 words   **Time taken** _____

Reading Comprehension

Choose the correct answers for the following questions.

1 The purpose of this passage is to _____ .
   a tell people why they shouldn't use cell phones or the Internet
   b discuss the benefits of email and real mail
   c explain how people use cell phones and the Internet
   d show how technology has improved our lives

2 Meredith dislikes using email because _____ .
   a they take too long to write
   b sending them wastes electricity
   c people do not read them carefully
   d she doesn't think it's polite to send email

3 What's one way in which Meredith expresses herself with her letters?
   a She makes her own envelopes.
   b She sends her friends interesting magazine articles.
   c She sends a photo of herself in her letters.
   d She uses her favorite black pen to write.

4 Why did Thomas start to send so much email?
   a He didn't have time to write letters.
   b He thought he was wasting too much paper.
   c He has to send a lot of mail for work.
   d He didn't have time to buy stamps.

5 Thomas likes using email because _____ .
   a it shows that the writer is being thoughtful
   b he doesn't trust the regular mail
   c it is the original way to keep in touch
   d it's easy and fast

6 Which is a benefit of both email and real mail?
   a You can keep in touch with friends.
   b You can save paper and energy.
   c You can write them both using your phone.
   d They make communication more interesting.

Turn to page 176 to record your reading fluency progress. First, find the vertical line that is closest to your reading rate. Next, how many of the six comprehension questions did you answer correctly? Find the point on the graph where your reading rate and your comprehension score meet. Mark that spot with a dot.
Which quadrant does the dot fall in? Your goal is to be a fluent reader and score in quadrant four.

Review Reading 4: Selecting the Olympic Sports

Fluency Practice

Time yourself as you read through the passage. Write your time in the space at the bottom of the page. Then answer the questions on the next page.

Selecting the Olympic Sports

During each Summer Olympic Games, 28 different sports are played. The kinds of sports played at the Olympics don't change very often, and the process for changing them is long and difficult. So it came as
5 a big surprise in 2005 when the International Olympic Committee (IOC) announced that it wanted to add new sports to the Summer Olympic Games. At that time, the list of sports hadn't changed in 70 years.

At a meeting in Singapore in 2005, the IOC voted on each of the 28 events from the 2004
10 Olympic Games in Athens, Greece. They wanted to choose which sports would be played at the 2016 games. There are many reasons why some sports make the list while others don't, but it's important that these sports are popular around the world, and played in many different countries.

The committee decided that baseball and softball would be replaced. Their new options included roller skating, rugby, golf, squash, and karate. To be included in the Olympics, a sport must 15 receive votes from at least two-thirds of the committee. The IOC had to meet more than once to come to a conclusion. Finally, in 2009, the results were announced: rugby and golf were the newest Olympic sports.

Both rugby and golf have 20 been Olympic sports before. Golf was part of the 1904 games over a century ago, and rugby was last played in the 1924 games. Now, both sports will rejoin
25 the Olympics for the 2016 Summer Games in Rio de Janeiro, Brazil.

Athletes from both sports are excited. New Zealand rugby star Jonah Lomu said, "(It's) just fantastic for the game." Golf superstar Jack Nicklaus feels just as
30 strongly. He says that "now people of all walks of life[1] will be inspired to play the game of golf, and play for sports' highest recognition. For all sports, that has always been a gold medal."

---

[1] People from all **walks of life** are people from different backgrounds, cultures, or positions in society.

335 words   **Time taken** _____

Reading Comprehension

Choose the correct answers for the following questions.

1 This reading is mainly about _____ .
   a why baseball and softball are no longer Olympic sports
   b how two new Olympic sports were selected
   c how the IOC was formed
   d how the best Olympic athletes started their careers

2 Why was it surprising when the IOC announced plans to change the list of Olympic sports?
   a The list of sports rarely changes.
   b The list had been changed very recently.
   c No one wanted the list of sports to change.
   d The sports were the same as at the Athens Olympics.

3 Which of these statements is NOT true about baseball and softball?
   a They will be played at the 2016 Olympics.
   b They were played at the Athens Olympics in 2004.
   c They didn't receive enough IOC votes in Singapore.
   d The IOC had to vote for new sports to take their place.

4 In the last paragraph, the quote from Jack Nicklaus was probably included because _____ .
   a he's a member of the IOC
   b he knows a lot about the Olympics
   c he's an expert on golf
   d he won a gold medal at the Olympics

5 When did the IOC decide to include rugby and golf in the Olympics?
   a 2004
   b 2005
   c 2009
   d 2016

6 Which is probably a reason rugby and golf were voted in?
   a They are followed by many people around the world.
   b They are better sports than squash and karate.
   c They are able to inspire people to watch the Olympics.
   d The athletes in the sports are very famous.

Turn to page 176 to record your reading fluency progress. First, find the vertical line that is closest to your reading rate. Next, how many of the six comprehension questions did you answer correctly? Find the point on the graph where your reading rate and your comprehension score meet. Mark that spot with a dot.
Which quadrant does the dot fall in? Your goal is to be a fluent reader and score in quadrant four.

Great Structures

The Beijing International Airport is the largest in the world.

Japan's Akashi-Kaikyo Bridge is the longest suspension bridge in the world.

South Korea's Dadaepo Sunset Fountain of Dreams is the world's largest fountain.

The Galleria Vittorio Emanuele in Milan, Italy, is probably the oldest shopping mall in the world.

Getting Ready

Discuss the following questions with a partner.

1 Have you ever seen any of the structures in the pictures above?
2 What other great structures or buildings do you know? Which ones have you visited?
3 Are there any great structures or buildings in your country?

CHAPTER 1 The World's Oldest Universities

Before You Read
The World's Oldest Universities

Cambridge University

TsingHua University

Harvard University

A Think about answers to the following questions.

1 Do you know these universities? Which countries are they in?
2 Can you think of other famous universities? How old do you think they are?
3 What universities are in your country? How old do you think they are?

B Discuss your answers with a partner.

Reading Skill
Identifying Supporting Details

A paragraph is often organized around a main point, which is often stated in the first sentence, and the details that support this point follow in the paragraph. In this passage, details are given about three different universities.

A How old are the following universities? Scan the passage on the next page and write the years in the table.

Name	Year founded	Location	Detail
University of Al-Karaouine			
Nalanda University			
University of Bologna			

B Scan the passage again to find the location, and one extra detail, about each university. Complete the chart.

Set a standard of respect. We all learn better when we are in a completely supportive learning environment. Students can build a supportive learning environment by showing respect for everyone in the class. As a class, talk about ways you can create a supportive and respectful classroom.

The World's Oldest Universities

Many universities around the world are proud to have long histories and strong traditions. However, very few universities can **claim** to be among the oldest in the world.

5

10

Nalanda University, in Bihar, India, was **established** around 600 BC. It was most likely the world's first university. In the past, scholars[1] came from Europe, China, and all over India to learn about science, medicine, the Buddhist religion, and other subjects. The university is in ruins now, but at one time it was an impressive school with temples, classrooms, libraries, and dormitories.[2]

According to the *Guinness Book of World Records*, the University of Al-Karaouine in Fes, Morocco, is the oldest **surviving** university
15 in the world. It was probably **founded** in 859 and became a famous place to study natural sciences. In 1957, after more than 1,000 years as a university, Al-Karaouine added mathematics, physics, chemistry, and various foreign languages
20 to its traditional list of **subjects** for study.

25

The first university in Europe is definitely the University of Bologna, in Italy. It was one of the few universities in Europe that were not influenced by religion. Professors were **forbidden** from teaching outside the university, and so students came from all over Europe to study with its famous teachers. Since opening in 1088, the University of Bologna has never closed its doors, **despite** the many wars in Europe.

30 With the success of the University of Bologna, other universities opened across Europe. They were started by kings, religious groups, and **former** professors. Today there are so many universities that students don't need to go far to study. They are sure to find one close to home.

---

[1] A **scholar** is a person who studies in school at a high level.
[2] A **dormitory** is a place for students to live.

Reading Comprehension
Check Your Understanding

A **Choose the correct answers for the following questions.**

1 Scholars came to Nalanda University to study _____.
   a math, art, and history
   b Buddhism, science, and medicine
   c geography, health, and philosophy

2 Al-Karaouine is said to be the _____.
   a oldest university in India
   b oldest surviving university
   c first university in Europe

3 Which university is no longer standing today?
   a University of Al-Karaouine
   b Nalanda University
   c University of Bologna

B **Read the following sentences. Check (✔) true (T) or false (F). If the sentence is false, change it to make it true.**

		T	F
1	Many universities can claim to be among the oldest in the world.		
2	Scholars came from all over India, Europe, and China to learn at Nalanda University.		
3	Mathematics is one of the oldest subjects taught at the University of Al-Karaouine.		
4	The only time the University of Bologna closed was during the wars in Europe.		
5	More universities opened because of the success of University of Bologna.		

Critical Thinking

C **Discuss the following questions with a partner.**

1 Do you think old universities are better than new universities? Why, or why not?
2 Before universities, how do you think people passed down knowledge?

Vocabulary Comprehension
Words in Context

A **Complete each statement with the best answer. The words in blue are from the passage.**

1 Which of these is forbidden in most classrooms?
   a smoking   b studying

2 Coach Jones is our former coach; he _____.
   a quit last year   b coaches us now

3 To claim to be the oldest means to _____ .
  a say that you are the oldest   b be the oldest
4 This building survived the earthquake. It must be very _____ .
  a strong   b weak
5 At school, her favorite subject was _____ .
  a history   b art club
6 Which can you establish?
  a a club   b a meal
7 If you found an organization, you _____ it.
  a close   b start
8 I did well on the exam despite _____ .
  a not studying for it   b studying a lot for it

B Answer the following questions, then discuss your answers with a partner. The words in blue are from the passage.

1 What did your parents forbid you to do when you were a child?
2 How long do you think a person can survive without food?
3 What have you managed to achieve despite lots of difficulties?
4 Which of your former teachers did you like the best? Why?

Read the words in the box. Which ones do you use when you're sure (S), and which do you use when you're unsure (U)? Write S or U next to each word.

Vocabulary Skill
Expressing Certainty

| _____ easily | _____ perhaps | _____ likely | _____ clearly |
| _____ probably | _____ possibly | _____ for sure | |

> When you write, you can add adverbs to show how sure you are. You can use adverbs like *definitely* when you are absolutely sure of information, and use adverbs like *unlikely* when you are not at all sure.

A Read the following sentences. Then decide if the writer of the following statements is sure (S) or unsure (U) about the information. Check (✔) your answer.

		S	U
1	Nalanda University is most likely the world's first university.		
2	The University of Al-Karaouine in Fes, Morocco, was probably founded in 859.		
3	The first university in Europe is definitely the University of Bologna, in Italy.		

B Now complete the sentences below using your own ideas.

1 In 50 years, cars will most likely _____ .
2 When I finish school today, I will definitely _____ .
3 In 100 years, money will possibly _____ .

CHAPTER 2 Modern Engineering Wonders

Before You Read
Great Engineering

A **Think about answers to the following questions.**

1 Do you recognize any of these structures?

2 What do you think they are? What do we use them for?

B **Discuss your answers with a partner.**

Reading Skill
Scanning

When we scan, we look for specific information. We scan a newspaper for sections we want to read, for example, or we scan to find information for a test. Passages or webpages with sections that have subheads can be easier to scan.

A **Scan the passage on the next page for five subheadings. Write the letters of the pictures above next to the correct structure in the following chart.**

Engineering wonder	Picture	Location
1 Falkirk Wheel		
2 Millau Viaduct		
3 Langeled Pipeline		
4 Three Gorges Dam		
5 Venice Tide Barrier		

B **Now scan the passage to find the location of these structures and write them in the chart.**

C **Read the entire passage carefully. Then answer the questions on page 94.**

Modern Engineering Wonders

*Great **Engineering*** has selected five wonders of 21st **century** engineering for our Excellence **Prize**. Now we're asking you to vote for one and tell us why!

Falkirk Wheel (Falkirk, Scotland, 2001)

The Falkirk Wheel is the world's only **rotating** boat lift. Its steel arms each hold a water-filled tank into which boats can sail. As the wheel rotates, so do the arms, raising and lowering the boats a distance of 25 meters. The wheel is very energy **efficient**, using about two kilowatt-hours to make a full rotation. That's about the same amount of energy needed to power a microwave for three minutes.

Millau Viaduct (Millau, France, 2005)

The 2.46-kilometer-long Millau Viaduct over the River Tam in the south of France is 270 meters high—the highest bridge in the world. It was built in just three years! It is an amazing bridge that adds to the **natural** beauty of the river valley.

Langeled Pipeline (The North Sea, 2007)

This pipeline[1] under the ocean carries natural gas across the 1,200 kilometers of rocky sea bed from Norway to Britain. It is the longest pipeline of its kind, and it helps supply 20 percent of Britain's gas.

Three Gorges Dam (Yichang, China, 2008)

Three Gorges Dam is the largest dam for electric power in the world. Its 1.6-kilometer-long wall across the Yangtze River rises 183 meters above the valley floor. It can hold back 39 million cubic meters of water.

Venice Tide Barrier (Venice, Italy, estimated 2014)

In 1966, the city of Venice was **flooded** in two meters of ocean water. To prevent this from happening again, the Italian government is building 78 walls, each about 600 square meters. When the water level of the Adriatic Sea reaches to a dangerous level and **threatens** to flood the city, the walls will rise to protect it.

[1] A **pipeline** is a long pipe that carries oil, gas, etc. a long distance.

Reading Comprehension
Check Your Understanding

A Choose the best answer for the following questions.

1 What does the Falkirk Wheel do?
  a It moves boats from one place to another.
  b It moves water using its steel arms.
  c It creates energy by making rotations.

2 What is true of the Venice Tide Barrier?
  a It is built to solve a recent problem.
  b It is 600 square meters large in total.
  c It only rises when there is a flood.

3 Which of the following is probably NOT a reason the structures were selected?
  a They were very difficult to design and build.
  b They were built in a very short space of time.
  c They are very useful to human beings.

B Read the following sentences. Check (✔) whether they are true for the Falkirk Wheel (F), Millau Viaduct (M), Langeled Pipeline (L), Three Gorges Dam (T), or Venice Tide Barrier (V).

This structure...	F	M	L	T	V
helps to control water.					
is built over a river.					
provides for people's energy needs.					
is the newest engineering wonder.					
is the only one of its kind.					
is the biggest/highest/longest of its kind.					

Critical Thinking

C Discuss the following questions with a partner.

1 What challenges did the engineers have building these structures?
2 What are examples of excellent engineering in your city or town? Why?

Vocabulary Comprehension
Words in Context

A Complete each statement with the best answer. The words in blue are from the passage.

1 He's so efficient. He _____ finished his work.
  a still hasn't   **b** has already

2 How many years are there in a century?
  a 100   **b** 1,000

3 Someone trained in engineering is able to _____.
  a build bridges   **b** make clothes

4 The whole area is flooded because it _____ heavily yesterday.
  a rained   **b** snowed

5 In a competition, a prize is given to _____ .

    a the winner   **b** the audience

6 A rotating sign goes _____ .

    a round and round   **b** up and down

7 If someone threatens you, they say they want to _____ .

    a hurt you   **b** give you a present

8 I think those pearls are natural. They were _____ .

    a fished from the sea   **b** made in a factory

B **Complete the following sentences using the words in blue from A. You might have to change the form of the word.**

1 She's a(n) _____ athlete. She didn't train much for the race and still won first _____ !

2 The broken water pipe _____ my bathroom.

3 The United States has been a country for more than two _____ .

4 The teacher _____ to report the student if he was late for class again.

A **There are a few rules to follow when forming superlatives. Look at the examples below.**

When an adjective …	You…	Examples	
a has one syllable	add -est	tall → tallest	neat → neatest
b ends in -e	add -st	nice → nicest	large → largest
c has one syllable and has consonant-vowel-consonant pattern	double the last consonant and add -est	big → biggest	thin → thinnest
d has two or more syllables and ends in -y	change the –y to i and add -est	pretty → prettiest easy → easiest	
e has two or more syllables and does not end in -y	put *the most* before it	curious → the most curious expensive → the most expensive	
f Note that some common adjectives have irregular superlative forms.		good → the best bad → the worst far → the farthest	

Vocabulary Skill
Superlatives

When we want to compare one thing or person to all the others in a group, we use the superlative form of an adjective. For example, *the tallest building in the world* or *the youngest person in this class*. Superlatives can be formed in different ways. Many often have *the* in front of them.

B **Look at the adjectives below. Write the letter (*a* to *f*) of the rule you would follow to form the superlative next to each word.**

1 ___ delicious   **5** ___ important   **9** ___ exciting   **13** ___ rude

2 ___ funny   **6** ___ useful   **10** ___ valuable   **14** ___ convenient

3 ___ large   **7** ___ angry   **11** ___ long   **15** ___ hot

4 ___ messy   **8** ___ simple   **12** ___ bad   **16** ___ high

C **Write three sentences using superlatives. Then read them to a partner.**

Real Life Skill

Recognizing Survey Question Types

Many organizations make surveys to collect information about people's views and opinions. These polls or surveys are organized in different ways. Knowing some of the different types of surveys used can help you to understand them better.

A Look at the three different survey question types about leisure activities. Match each question to its type in the box below by writing 1-3.

1 Check (✓) the activities you like doing.

_____ watching movies   _____ cooking

_____ reading   _____ listening to music

2 Number the following activities 1 (most) to 4 (least) in the order you like doing them.

_____ watching movies   _____ cooking

_____ reading   _____ listening to music

3 Which one of the following is your favorite leisure activity?

a watching movies   **c** cooking

b reading   **d** listening to music

_____ order of preference   _____ multiple choice   _____ item selection

B Internet Challenge: Look for examples of survey question types online. If possible, print out examples. Present the information to the class.

C Prepare your own survey using some or all of the survey question types above. Remember to pick a topic that your classmates will be interested in answering questions about.

What do you think?

1 The Seven Wonders of the World are considered the world's greatest structures. Can you name them? Where are they located?

2 What differences can you think of between building a structure today and building one a hundred years ago? How about a thousand years ago?

3 Why do you think humans choose to build these great structures? What other purpose do they serve?

Learn inside and outside of the classroom. If possible, organize an extracurricular activity where you can learn more about the topic outside of the classroom. After the activity, identify three ways that the extracurricular activity helped you learn better.

ZDRAVSTVUITE!

Bom dia! *Aloha!*

Nǐ **Bonjour!**

hǎo! *Konnichiwa!*

Guten tag! ▲**Annyong ha shimnikka!**

¡Hola! **Namasté!**

Getting Ready

Discuss the following questions with a partner.

1 Look at the ways to say *Hello* in the different languages above. Which ones do you know?
2 How many languages can you speak? Which languages would you like to learn?
3 Which are the most popular languages to study in your country? Why are they popular?

CHAPTER 1 Which English Will We Speak?

Before You Read
Languages Without
Borders

A Match each group of countries to the language they share.

1	_____	Austria, Germany, Liechtenstein	a	Portuguese
2	_____	Egypt, Syria, Yemen	b	Spanish
3	_____	Chile, Colombia, Cuba	c	Arabic
4	_____	Brazil, Cape Verde, Portugal	d	English
5	_____	Australia, Barbados, Jamaica	e	German

B Answer the following questions.

1 Why do we learn English? Why do you think English is a popular language to learn?

2 Do you know of any differences between the English spoken in countries like the U.S., England, and Australia? Give some examples.

C Discuss your answers with a partner.

Reading Skill
Identifying Main Ideas

When we read, we try to make connections between what we are reading and what we already know. It is easier to make those connections if we know the main idea of the text.

A Skim each paragraph of the passage on the next page. Then match each paragraph to its main idea.

1	_____	Paragraph 1	4	_____	Paragraph 4
2	_____	Paragraph 2	5	_____	Paragraph 5
3	_____	Paragraph 3			

a There are many varieties of English.
b The future of English is uncertain.
c English is widely used and growing in countries like China and Russia.
d The first group consists of countries with native English speakers.
e Countries like India and Malaysia use their own variety of English in everyday life.

B Skim the passage again quickly. Then complete the sentence below.

The main idea of this passage is that _____.
a the most important type of English continues to be British English
b there are many types of English, and they will continue to change
c English will not be the international language for much longer

C Now read the entire passage carefully. Then answer the questions on page 100.

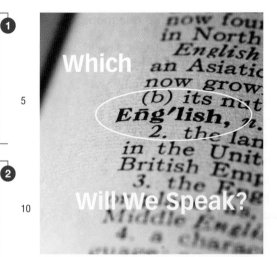

Which Will We Speak?

English is called an international language, but there are actually quite a few **varieties** of English that **exist** around the world. English **originated** in England, but soon English spread to other countries, and different varieties of English began to exist. Today, the countries in which English is spoken can be divided into three groups.

The first group is made of those countries where English is the **primary** language. These are countries like England, Canada, the United States, Ireland, Australia, and New Zealand. There are more than 380 million native[1] speakers of English in these countries alone.

There is a second group of countries that have their own varieties of English. Their histories have been directly influenced by one of the early English-speaking societies. They use English in various important ways within their own government and everyday life. India, Malaysia, the Philippines, and Kenya are examples of this group. The total number of speakers in this group is in the hundreds of millions.

In a third group of countries, English is widely used as a foreign language. However, citizens use their native language within their own government and in everyday life. Some countries in this group are China, Russia, Japan, Korea, Brazil, Indonesia, and many Western European countries. Some people **calculate** the number of speakers in this group to be as many as one billion—and it is growing fast.

This changing **situation** raises many questions. Will another language **replace** English as the international language? If not, will people continue to use the English of countries such as England or the United States as models? Will new varieties of English **develop** in countries such as China or Brazil? Or, in the future, will a new international variety of English develop that doesn't belong to any one country, but to an entire area like Asia or Europe?

---

[1] Your **native** language is the first language you learned to speak.

Reading Comprehension
Check Your Understanding

A **Choose the correct answers for the following questions.**

1 England, America, Canada, Ireland, Australia, and New Zealand are countries where _____.
   a people speak English as a foreign language
   b English is the main language
   c people still use the type of English used in England

2 In China and Brazil, English is widely used _____.
   a in everyday life
   b by the government
   c as a foreign language

3 The _____ group has the most number of English speakers.
   a first
   b second
   c third

4 Which sentence is the writer most likely to agree with?
   a English will stay in its current form for a long time.
   b No one knows if English will remain the international language.
   c Soon there will be more native speakers of English than non-native speakers.

B **Read the following sentences. Check (✓) true (T), false (F), or not given (NG). If the sentence is false, change it to make it true.**

	T	F	NG
1 English originated in the United States.			
2 The writer thinks English is easy to learn.			
3 The Philippines has its own variety of English.			
4 English is widely used as a foreign language in Egypt.			

Critical Thinking

C **Discuss the following questions with a partner.**

1 Do you think it is important for the world to have an international language? Why, or why not?

2 Do you think another language will replace English as the international language in the future? Why, or why not?

Effort versus ability. Did you make mistakes on the comprehension checks in this unit because of a lack of effort or because the items are beyond your ability level? Many learners want to blame mistakes on lack of ability, but often our mistakes are a result of not trying hard enough.

A Match each word with its definition. The words in blue are from the passage.

1 _____ exist   **a** to work with numbers
2 _____ calculate   **b** to grow or change over time
3 _____ primary   **c** how things are
4 _____ develop   **d** begin
5 _____ originate   **e** type or kind of something
6 _____ replace   **f** the main or most important thing
7 _____ situation   **g** to take or fill the place of
8 _____ variety   **h** to be real or to be present

B Complete the following sentences using the correct form of words from **A**.

1 I'm terrible at math. It takes me forever to _____ my expenses.
2 I need a new pair of shoes to _____ my old ones, but there's such a big _____ that I can't decide which to buy!
3 It can be an uncomfortable _____ when you forget someone's name.
4 The city _____ slowly along the river, which became its _____ source of water.

A Look at these English words that came from other languages. Practice saying them with a partner. Can you add any more to the chart?

Language	Loan word
French	passport
Turkish	kiosk
Latin	candle
Italian	violin
Spanish	mosquito
German	hamburger

Language	Loan word
Dutch	cruise
Indian	shampoo
Japanese	tsunami
Malay	ketchup
Chinese	tea
Inuit	kayak

> There are many words in English that have come from other languages. These are called *loan words* and they are now used as part of everyday English.

B Complete the following sentences using the correct form of the words in **A**. You may use your dictionary to help you.

1 Would you like some coffee or _____?
2 A _____ is a very small animal that drinks blood.
3 I'm using a new _____. It makes my hair really shiny.
4 I would like some _____ on my _____.
5 You have to bring your _____ with you when you go traveling.
6 I bought a magazine at the _____.
7 The _____ in 2004 destroyed many areas near the Indian Ocean.
8 I wish I had learned to play the _____ when I was younger.

CHAPTER 2 Sign Language

A This is the alphabet for American Sign Language. Practice making these signs with your hand.

SIGN LANGUAGE

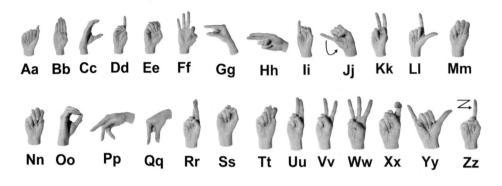

Aa Bb Cc Dd Ee Ff Gg Hh Ii Jj Kk Ll Mm

Nn Oo Pp Qq Rr Ss Tt Uu Vv Ww Xx Yy Zz

B Use the sign language above to spell English words to a partner.

Reading Skill
Distinguishing Main Idea and Supporting Details

> Many paragraphs have a main idea that is supported by a number of details. Not all details in a paragraph support the main idea; some support the supporting ideas themselves. Finding the main and most important supporting idea helps us clearly understand the writer's point.

A Read the first paragraph of the passage on the next page. Then look at the main idea and one supporting idea below. Add two more supporting details.

Main idea: Deaf people have special ways of communicating.

Supporting details:

1 _____

2 It is possible for deaf people to speak with special voice training.

3 _____

B Now read the second paragraph of the passage. Then write the main idea and three supporting details.

Main idea: _____

1 _____

2 _____

3 _____

C Read the entire passage carefully. Then answer the questions on page 104.

1 Because deaf people cannot hear, they have special ways of **communicating**. For example, they can learn to understand what someone is saying by looking at the mouth of the speaker. This is called lipreading. Also, speaking is very difficult for the deaf, because they cannot hear their own voices. However, it is possible
5 with special training. According to many deaf people all around the world, the most **practical** and popular way of communicating is with sign language.

2 In many ways, sign language is **similar** to spoken language. The words of sign language are made with signs, which are formed with movements of the hands, face, and body. As with words, each sign has a different meaning and can be
10 combined to form sentences. Signed languages also have their own grammar. The alphabet of sign language is special hand signs that **stand for** letters; they make spelling possible. The signs combine to form a rich language that can express the same thoughts, feelings, and ideas as any spoken language. And just as people from different countries speak different languages, most countries have their own
15 variety of sign language.

3 In addition to knowing sign language, it is also helpful to know something about how deaf people communicate. Since they rely so much on actions, deaf people are
20 generally not very **formal** when they "talk," and may touch your arm or shoulder a lot to make sure you know what they're saying. It is not seen as rude among deaf people to lightly touch someone you do

25 not know to get their attention. It's also okay to wave your hands or hit the table or floor. Also, lots of eye contact[1] is necessary.

4 There are many ways to learn a few signs. Community colleges often teach **introductory** classes. For self-learners, bookstores and libraries have books for learning sign language. There are also instructional[2] videos on the Internet, with
30 actors **demonstrating** signs and performing interesting stories and conversations for you to see. With practice, you'll soon **get the hang of** this useful method of communicating!

[1] If you make **eye contact** with someone, you look into their eyes.
[2] Something **instructional** is full of information, or for learning.

Reading Comprehension

Check Your Understanding

A **Complete the following summary using words from the passage.**

Deaf people have special ways of communicating. While they can't hear, they also find it hard to speak because they cannot hear their **(1)** _____.
Some deaf people use **(2)** _____, where they watch the speaker's mouth. But the most widely-used method of communication is **(3)** _____.
They use hand signs to spell letters of the **(4)** _____, and use hand and body movements to form words and sentences. They even have their own **(5)** _____ in the same way people in different countries speak different languages. In addition to hand signs, communicating with deaf people involves a lot of touching and making **(6)** _____. You may also have to wave your hands or **(7)** _____ the table or floor to get their attention. There are lots of ways to learn sign language. You can go for **(8)** _____ with trained teachers, read **(9)** _____ about it, or watch **(10)** _____. All it takes is effort and practice!

B **Read the following sentences. Check (✓) true (T) or false (F) or Not Given (NG). If the sentence is false, change it to make it true.**

		T	F	NG
1	You can learn to lipread by reading a book.			
2	Lots of eye contact is necessary for deaf people.			
3	Sign language has letters, but no words.			
4	Waving your hands at someone is considered rude by deaf people.			

Critical Thinking

C **Discuss the following questions with a partner.**

1 Think of all the things you do in an average day. Which ones wouldn't you do if you were deaf?
2 How would you design alarm clocks, doorbells, and telephones for deaf people?

Vocabulary Comprehension

Words in Context

A **Complete each statement with the best answer. The words in blue are from the passage.**

1 When you get the hang of something, it becomes much _____.
  a easier   **b** harder
2 Practical advice is useful _____.
  a on special occasions   **b** in everyday life
3 Which words below are similar?
  a big, small   **b** small, short
4 What do _____ stand for?
  a the numbers 123   **b** the letters ATM

5 He'll demonstrate the move. You just have to _____ him.
   a watch   **b** listen to
6 In an introductory class, you will probably learn _____ from the
   teacher.
   a simple information   **b** advanced information
7 Which of the following involves communication?
   a writing, typing   **b** running, jumping
8 Who would you send a formal letter to?
   a your close friend   **b** your boss

**B Answer the following questions, then discuss your answers with a
partner. The words in blue are from the passage.**

1 What occasions are generally seen as formal?
2 How are you similar to people in your family?
3 What letters do you know that stand for something?
4 What are some ways that animals communicate?

**A Complete the chart with the missing parts of speech. Use your
dictionary to help you. Compare your answers with a partner.**

Noun	Verb	Adjective
1		introductory
2 variety		
3	threaten	
4	imagine	
5 harm		
6		communicative

**B Complete the following sentences using the correct form of the words
from the chart.**

1 Smoking can be very _____ to your health.
2 The band sang a _____ of songs during the performance.
3 He must have a great _____ to come up with that crazy story!
4 The robber _____ to hurt me if I didn't give him my wallet.
5 The first chapter of *Dancing Today* is a great _____ to modern
   dance.
6 Couples who _____ with each other usually have a happy
   marriage.

Vocabulary Skill
Word Families

When you learn a
new word in English,
it is helpful to also
learn words that are
related to it. Learning
the different parts
of speech that form
the word family can
help you expand your
vocabulary.

Real Life Skill
Distinguishing American and British Words

There can be many differences in language even between two English-speaking countries like the U.S. and England. Aside from differences in spelling, certain terms are used in England, and countries using British English, which may be foreign to Americans and countries that use American English, although they may refer to the same thing.

A Do you know the following words? Match the words from the box to their American or British counterparts.

petrol	toilet	cookies	truck	flat
elevator	rubbish	queue	soccer	pants

American	British
line	
	football
	biscuits
gas	
	lorry
restroom	
apartment	
	trousers
trash	
	lift

B Discuss your answers with a partner. Then answer the following questions.

1 Which of these words are more commonly used in your country?
2 Can you think of any more British and American English words which refer to the same thing?

Create realistic learner beliefs. Do you have certain beliefs about what it takes to be a good reader? Some of them may be unrealistic or even incorrect. Write down two beliefs you have about reading, and discuss them as a class. How can you adjust some of these beliefs to fit your learning needs?

What do you think?

1 Do you think technology has changed the way we communicate? How?
2 Do you think there will be more or less languages in the future? Why?
3 Does English make a good or a bad international language? Why?

Festivals and Celebrations

Mardi Gras, Brazil

Los Sanfermines, Spain

Jaipur Elephant Festival, India

Thanksgiving Parade, the United States

Getting Ready

Discuss the following questions with a partner.

1 What is happening in each of the pictures?
2 Which of the festivals above do you know about? What do you know about them?
3 What is your favorite festival? Why do you like it?

CHAPTER 1 How Do You Celebrate?

Before You Read
Unique Festivals

A Which countries celebrate these festivals? Match the country to the festival.

> Thailand   England   India   Spain   Mexico

1 **Day of the Dead:** People pray for the dead, and decorate graves with food, candles, and flowers. They also dress up as skeletons and bake bread in the shape of skulls. _____

2 **La Tomatina:** People gather to throw thousands of tomatoes at each other in the town square. _____

3 **Holi:** Participants sing and dance, and throw colored powders and water at each other. _____

4 **Songkran:** People try to soak each other using containers of water or water guns. They might also hide with garden hoses to splash people.

_____

5 **Cheese Rolling Festival:** Each year, an official throws blocks of cheese down a very steep hill, and participants chase and try to catch them.

_____

B Discuss your answers with a partner. What other unique festivals do you know?

Reading Skill
Scanning

> When we scan, we look for information that we want and ignore other information. On tests, scanning can be useful when checking if a fact is true or false, or to find the place in a passage about which a question is asked.

A Read the expressions below. (Circle) the best word(s) to complete each expression.

1 (tell / share / say) goodbye
2 (have / make / teach) a promise
3 (use / lose / spend) weight
4 (all / most / total) night
5 (get / take / receive) place
6 (enter / jump / join) the party
7 (get / take / have) together

B Now scan the passage on the next page to find the expressions and check your answers.

C Read the entire passage carefully. Then answer the questions on page 110.

> **Set high expectations for yourself.** Keep your learning goals high. Stay focused on your professional and personal goals for learning English. If you do, it will be easier to achieve them.

How Do You Celebrate?

New Year's Day

New Year is one of the most popular **festivals** in the world, even though it is **celebrated** at different times and in different ways. In many western countries, people get together with
5 family and friends on December 31 to eat, drink, and dance as they wait for January 1. Some of the biggest parties are held on New Year's Eve. In many cities, crowds gather in the center of town to welcome the new year at midnight with fireworks.

For many Asian countries like China, Taiwan, and Vietnam,
10 the New Year is based on a lunar calendar.[1] The date changes from year to year, but usually falls between January 21 and February 21. It is traditionally seen as a time for family **reunions**, with people traveling across the country and from overseas. Many people wear red clothes, as it is thought to be a lucky color. They also give "lucky money" in red
15 envelopes to friends and family, and set off firecrackers[2] to scare away bad luck.

What's common among these celebrations is the meaning of the new year; it is a time to say goodbye to the past and to think about new beginnings. For example, in Japan, people organize *bonenkai* parties ("year forgetting parties"), which are **dedicated to** leaving the old year's worries and troubles behind. In many countries, people make New
20 Year's resolutions—promises to themselves to make changes in their lives over the coming year, such as to lose weight, stop smoking, or learn a new skill.

Carnival

In late February or early March, some countries celebrate a special festival
25 called Carnival. Carnival is thought to have originated in Italy or Greece, and was held just before Lent, the 40-day period before Easter[3]. People dressed in costumes, wore colorful **masks**, ate, drank, and danced all night. This
30 tradition **spread** to France, Spain, Portugal, and later to Brazil and the United States.

Now, two of the biggest Carnival celebrations take place in Rio de Janeiro in Brazil, and New Orleans in the United States. There are grand **parades** where people wear **flashy** costumes and dance and sing in the streets.
35 In New Orleans, Carnival is known as Mardi Gras. Many roads and shops are shut down for the celebrations which can last for up to three weeks. Millions of visitors travel from around the world to join the party, and many more watch the event on television.

---

[1] A **lunar calendar** is based on the stages of the moon rather than the sun.
[2] A **firecracker** is a small paper case that can be exploded to make noise.
[3] **Easter** is a religious holiday for Christians.

Reading Comprehension
Check Your Understanding

A Read the following sentences. Check (✔) true (T) or false (F). If the sentence is false, change it to make it true.

		T	F
1	In many western countries, New Year starts after midnight on December 31.		
2	In some Asian countries, the new year starts on January 21 and ends on February 21.		
3	Red clothes and envelopes are said to bring good luck.		
4	Carnival is one of the days of Lent.		
5	The Mardi Gras is famous all over the world.		

B Read the following sentences. Check (✔) whether they are true for New Year (N), Carnival (C), or both.

		N	C
1	People have parties and celebrations in the streets.		
2	People get together with friends and family.		
3	This festival is celebrated all over the world.		
4	This festival can last up to three weeks.		
5	People make promises to themselves during this time.		
6	People wear brightly colored clothes.		

Critical Thinking

C Discuss the following questions with a partner.

1 Why do you think people need to welcome the start of the new year?
2 Why do you think festivals are important? What purpose do they serve?

Vocabulary Comprehension
Definitions

A Match each word with its definition. The words in blue are from the passage

1	_____ reunion	a	gives a lot of time and effort (to achieve something)
2	_____ spread	b	very bright and colorful
3	_____ mask	c	to have a party (for a happy reason)
4	_____ festival	d	this covers your face or eyes
5	_____ dedicated to	e	to move in many directions
6	_____ parade	f	a day or time of year when people celebrate a special event
7	_____ celebrate	g	a meeting between people who haven't seen each other for a long time
8	_____ flashy	h	people walking down the street together with music and costumes

B Complete the following sentences with the correct form of the words from **A**.

1 What is your family doing to _____ your sister's birthday?
2 I want to find a good spot to watch the _____; my daughter is in the marching band.
3 In the sport of fencing, people wear _____ to protect their face.
4 You should see the doctor before you _____ your illness to other people.

A Look at how different prepositions are used with different time expressions.

Use *in* with months, seasons, years, some parts of the day, and periods of time in the future

> *in December   in spring   in the morning   in 1975   in four months*
> Exception: *at night*

Use *on* with days of the week, specific dates, special days, and other time expressions

> *on Monday   on December 15   on Christmas Day   on the weekend*

Use *at* with exact times of day

> *at 10 o'clock   at noon*

Vocabulary Skill

Prepositions of Time: *in, on, at*

When we talk about time, we often use prepositions. The most common prepositions in expressions about time are *in, on,* and *at.* There are some basic rules for how to use them correctly.

B Complete the following sentences with *in, on,* and, *at.*

1 I have to take my cat to the vet _____ Friday.
2 I have to take my medicine _____ exactly 7:00. Don't let me forget!
3 We need to give him that report _____ February 12.
4 My summer course begins _____ two weeks.
5 I'll meet you at the café tonight _____ 7:30.
6 I graduated from university _____ October.
7 I paid a lot of taxes _____ 2006.

C Now complete these sentences about yourself. Use the correct time expressions.

1 My birthday is _____ _____.
2 I usually go on vacation _____ _____.
3 I usually eat breakfast _____ _____.
4 I typically go to bed _____ _____.
5 _____ New Year's Day I always _____.

CHAPTER 2 Edinburgh Festival Journal

Before You Read
Festivals

Festivals can be a series of activities, cultural events, or entertainment. They can also be events held by the local community, which celebrates some unique part of that community.

A Look at the kinds of festivals below and answer the following questions.

art   book   comedy   fashion
film   sports   music   food

1 Which kinds of festivals have you attended? Which ones would you like to attend?

2 What other kinds of festivals can you think of?

B Skim the journal on the next page. What kind of festival do you think it describes?

Reading Skill
Reading for Details

When reading for details, we read every word and make sure we understand the meaning. Reading for details is especially useful when we need to get information from one part of a larger reading. We can scan the passage for the part we need to read for details. We often need to do this when taking tests.

A Read the following sentences. Then scan the journal on the next page. Check (✔) three things that happened on September 2.

1 ☐ They had some delicious local food.

2 ☐ They watched a parade of actors.

3 ☐ They went to the Jazz & Blues Festival.

4 ☐ They went for a long walk.

5 ☐ They watched some short plays in the Fringe Festival.

6 ☐ They arrived in Edinburgh.

B Check (✔) three things they did on September 3.

1 ☐ They spent the afternoon walking along the river.

2 ☐ They watched a comedian peform.

3 ☐ They checked out of the hotel and went to the airport.

4 ☐ They watched fireworks.

5 ☐ They went to the Foodies Festival for dinner.

6 ☐ They took part in a painting class.

C Now read the entire passage carefully. Then answer the questions on page 114.

Humor and reading. What is the funniest thing you have read in the past week? Reading the comics can be a fun thing to read. Humor is often based on cultural issues. Reading and understanding humor in English can be a fun way to learn more.

Edinburgh Festival Journal

September 1

I'm so excited! My roommate Christopher and I are on our flight to Edinburgh, Scotland, for the Edinburgh International Festival. It's the biggest arts festival in the world and combines many

5 **separate** festivals happening at the same time. I'm **especially** excited to see lots of indie[1] art and films. There's so much to do, and we only have three days!

September 2

Christopher and I arrived at our hotel in Edinburgh last night. After **checking**

10 **in**, we had dinner and explored the city streets. It was really **fascinating** but we went to bed soon after because we were so tired! Today we went to King's Theater to watch some short plays that are part of the Fringe Festival. People here call it "The Fringe," and it has an awesome variety of shows by all sorts of performing arts groups. A parade of actors **greeted** us as we walked

15 down the street. They were waving colorful flags, one for each of the theater companies performing at the festival. It was a great way for us to start our festival experience. Christopher wants to hear some bands at the Jazz & Blues Festival, and we hope to see a good film tonight.

September 3

20 I saw an awesome comedian today! He was so funny that I couldn't stop laughing. I wish we had these kind of events in my hometown. Christopher and I spent the afternoon walking along the river. There were painters on either side, working and **displaying** all kinds of art. Later, we went

25 to the Foodies Festival for dinner and tried local Scottish foods. Most of it was delicious, although there were a few foods we didn't **dare** try—like haggis![2]

September 4

Today is the final day of the International Festival, but some of the smaller festivals will go on for a few

30 more days. The plan is to watch some short plays in the amphitheater in the park after lunch. Then, later tonight, we'll attend the closing **ceremonies** in the city center and watch the fireworks. I can't believe the festival is almost over!

---

[1] **Indie** is short for *independent* and describes an artistic work produced by a small company or group.
[2] **Haggis** is a kind of sausage made from the heart, liver, lungs, and stomach of a sheep.

Reading Comprehension
Check Your Understanding

A **Choose the best answer for the following questions.**

1 Christopher is the writer's _____ .
   a roommate   **b** student   **c** boss

2 After the writer and Christopher checked into the hotel, the first thing they did was _____ .
   a go to sleep   **b** have dinner   **c** see a play

3 The _____ made the writer laugh a lot.
   a amphitheater   **b** comedian   **c** local Scottish foods

4 Which of these is the main festival?
   a Fringe Festival
   b Jazz & Blues Festival
   c Edinburgh International Festival

B **Number these events (1–5) in the order they happened.**

a _____ The writer attended the closing ceremonies in the city center.
b _____ A parade of actors greeted the writer in the street.
c _____ The writer saw painters working and displaying all kinds of art.
d _____ The writer couldn't stop laughing at the comedian.
e _____ The writer attended the Foodies Festival.

Critical Thinking

C **Discuss the following questions with a partner.**

1 How do people in Scotland probably feel about the arts?
2 What do you think about a festival that brings together so many different arts? Would you like to go to this festival?

Vocabulary Comprehension
Odd Word Out

A **For each group, circle the word that does not belong. The words in blue are from the passage.**

1	interesting	fascinating	obvious
2	display	show	disguise
3	welcome	express	greet
4	hold back	dare	try
5	especially	normally	commonly
6	register	check in	fly in
7	separate	different	altogether
8	celebration	education	ceremony

B **Complete the following sentences using the words in blue from A. You might have to change the form of the word.**

1 He has pictures of his family _____ on his wall.
2 Would you ever _____ go sky-diving?
3 At the airport, we waited in a long line just to _____ .
4 My dog and cat sleep in _____ rooms, otherwise they will fight.

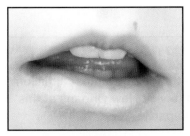

a taste

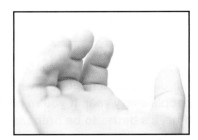

b touch

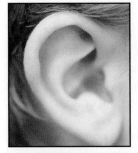

c hearing

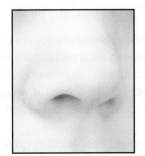

d smell

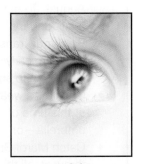

e sight

Vocabulary Skill
Sensory Verbs

The five senses are sight, sound, smell, taste, and touch. There are many verbs in English associated with each sense. They often have differences in meaning and are used in different ways. For example, you *watch TV*, but *look at a painting*.

A **Match the following verbs to the senses. Write the letter of the picture next to each verb.**

1 _____ listen
2 _____ watch
3 _____ hear
4 _____ smell
5 _____ lick
6 _____ touch

7 _____ taste
8 _____ look
9 _____ see
10 _____ feel
11 _____ sniff

B **Complete the following sentences with the correct verb from B above. Add prepositions like *at*, *to*, or *in* if you need to.**

1 There's a good movie on TV tonight. Do you want to _____ it?
2 We're going to _____ a Picasso exhibition at the museum.
3 This sauce doesn't _____ right. Maybe you should add more salt?
4 Do you _____ to the radio every morning? I can _____ music coming from your room.
5 You have to _____ this cloth to _____ how soft it is.

Real Life Skill

Reading Tourist Information

Many cities have a Visitors' Bureau or Tourist Information Center. They have brochures and websites with information about places to visit, sightseeing tours, festivals, and events. Understanding some of the language commonly used in this information can help you plan your trip better.

A   Read this brochure about a festival.

CELEBRATE MARDI GRAS IN NEW ORLEANS!

Mardi Gras is a huge festival and is attended by almost a million people every year. If you're planning to visit New Orleans at this time, it's better to be prepared for the party!

Tips for visitors:

- Plan ahead: Many hotels start taking reservations for Mardi Gras in August. To get the room you want, call well in advance. Don't wait until January!
- Plan your transportation: Many streets are closed to cars.
- Get there early: For the big parades on the weekend before Mardi Gras, plan to arrive about four hours ahead of time to find a good spot.
- Check the weather forecasts: It can be very warm or very cold at this time of year. You might need a jacket, sunscreen, or an umbrella—or all three.
- Catch Mardi Gras *throws*: People riding on floats in the parades throw small things to the crowd. Spectators jump up to catch beads, plastic coins, cups, and toy animals. Bring a plastic bag to hold all your souvenirs.

B   Match each word in blue in the brochure with its meaning below.

1 a prediction of how the weather will be   _____
2 pieces of useful information   _____
3 an arrangement to confirm accommodation or seats _____
4 a long time before   _____
5 people who watch an event   _____
6 a small item to remind you of the place you visited _____

C   Read the following sentences. Check (✔) (T) or false (F). Then (circle) the information in the brochure that helped you find the answer.

		T	F
1	The weather is always good in New Orleans at this time of year.		
2	You should make hotel reservations for Mardi Gras in January.		
3	You can get lots of free souvenirs at the parades.		
4	All of the parades are held on one day.		

What do you think?

1 What are some holidays in your country? What do you do on those days?
2 Do you think festivals are more popular now or in the past? Why?

Review Unit 3

Fluency Strategy: Dealing with Unknown Words

If you stop to learn every new word you read, you will read less fluently. It is often possible to skip unknown words when you read.

A Read the first paragraph of the article on the next page. (Circle) any words you do not know. As you circle the words, don't stop—keep reading!

B Look at the words you circled and complete the chart below.

Unknown word	Line number	Unknown word	Line number

Did you circle any word more than once? If a new word comes up several times, then it may be important to learn that word. For example, the word *submarine* appears four times. Do you already know what it means? If not, can you guess its meaning in the first paragraph?

C Now answer this comprehension question about the paragraph you just read:

What is NOT true about the submarine Shinkai 6500?
a   It has never been used outside Japan.
b   Three people can ride in it.
c   It can dive deeper than other submarines.
d   It is 9.5 meters long.

Were you able to answer this question without looking up the meaning of the unknown word(s)? Remember, you don't always need to understand every word to understand the meaning of the passage.

D Now read the entire article, without using a dictionary. (Circle) any words you don't know, but don't worry about their meaning. How many words did you skip?

Complete the chart below.

Unknown word	Line number	Unknown word	Line number

Amazing Machines!

The deepest diving submarine

The Japanese research submarine Shinkai 6500 can dive deeper than any other submarine. On August 11, 1989, it went down to a depth of 6,526 meters beneath the ocean's surface. The submarine is 9.5 meters long, about the size of a bus and can take up to three people. It is used for ocean research all over the world.

The world's most intelligent vacuum cleaner

The iRobot vacuum cleaner can clean your floor by itself. It has computers to help it see and hear, so it can detect walls and stairs. It even knows which part of the floor is dirtiest. It cleans the floor in three stages. First, it picks up dirt and pet hair, then it puts them into a special bin. Finally, the machine cleans the air, making the room fresher and healthier!

The most useful television

The Viera is the name of the world's only digital entertainment device that can go underwater. It is made and sold in Japan. You can listen to your favorite music, or even watch a movie, all from the comfort of your bathtub. And the battery lasts over five hours if you're planning to spend a long time bathing. You can even use headphones with it—all you'll need is to find a pair that is waterproof!

The smartest monitor

The Japanese company Eizo Nanao has invented a very special computer monitor, called the FlexScan monitor. The FlexScan monitor can stand up to 23 centimeters high, and it can turn almost 180 degrees left or right. It weighs only 4.3 kilograms. What's more, it can help save electricity. It senses when you have left your computer and turns itself off when you've been gone for more than 40 seconds. When you come back, it knows to turns itself back on!

The smallest motorcycle

A Swedish man named Tom Wiberg built the world's smallest motorcycle that can be ridden by a person. He calls it the Small Toe. The front wheel is only 1.6 centimeters wide, and the back wheel is 2.2 centimeters wide. The rider sits barely seven centimeters above the ground. In 2003, Wiberg rode his machine for more than ten meters and set a new Guinness World Record for the smallest rideable motorcycle ever built.

Reading Comprehension

Choose the correct answers for the following questions.

1 What can the iRobot vacuum cleaner clean?
   a walls
   b air
   c pets
   d computers

2 According to the passage, why is the Viera special?
   a It plays very loud music.
   b It is made in Japan.
   c Its battery lasts five hours.
   d You can use it underwater.

3 Why is the FlexScan monitor "smart"?
   a It knows when you leave your computer.
   b It can turn almost 180 degrees.
   c It cleans the air in the room.
   d It can be used underwater.

4 Wiberg probably made the world's smallest motorcycle _____.
   a for the police
   b to sell to Swedish motorcycle riders
   c because he wanted to set a new record
   d as a way to travel around the city

5 Which machine would a deep-sea photographer probably use?
   a Shinkai 6500
   b iRobot
   c Viera
   d FlexScan

6 What is true about all the machines in the reading?
   a They are very small.
   b They contain computers.
   c They are unique in some way.
   d You can buy them in stores.

SELF CHECK

Answer the following questions.

1 Look again at the vocabulary learning tips on pages 6–7. Which of these tips do you think is most useful? Why?

_____

_____

2 What do you usually do when you find a word you don't know?

_____

_____

3 Do you think that you can still understand a passage if you skip some unknown words? Why, or why not?

_____

_____

4 Which of the six reading passages in Units 7–9 did you enjoy most? Why?

_____

_____

5 Which of the six reading passages in Units 7–9 was easiest? Which was most difficult? Why?

_____

_____

6 What have you read in English outside of class recently?

_____

_____

7 What time of day is the best time for you to read and comprehend well? Do you use that part of the day to do your most important reading and studying?

_____

_____

8 Do you keep a vocabulary notebook? Why?

_____

Review Reading 5: Dying Languages

Dying Languages

The world is getting smaller, at least when it comes to language. More and more people speak the three most common languages: English, Spanish, and Mandarin. As a result, local languages are being forgotten. In many parts of the world, grandparents speak a language their grandchildren do not understand. As cultures adjust to these changes, and languages aren't taught to children or spoken at home, these local languages are slowly disappearing. 5

A language is said to be in trouble when less than 30 percent of children in the community speak it. It is considered a dying language. If children no longer learn to use a language, it will have fewer and fewer speakers over time and, eventually, the language will be gone. 10

Why keep languages alive? Languages hold the key to understanding a culture's beliefs and values. They show how a culture understands or explains the world. "You need to look at a variety of languages, because no one language gets it all," said anthropologist[1] Dr. Linda Cumberland who is working to save Assiniboine, a Native American language. 15 20

According to Dr. Cumberland, a dying language needs a dictionary and people to understand and record its grammar. Most importantly, you need to listen to those who still speak the language. This can be very difficult, especially if there are very few speakers of the language left. For example, when researchers were working to save the language Ayapaneco in Mexico, it was hard for them to record anything because the last two people on Earth who could speak the language refused to speak to each other! 25

Today, the United Nations Educational, Scientific and Cultural Organization (UNESCO) lists more than 3,000 languages that may disappear by the end of this century. Some of the languages still have a few million speakers and may survive. Unfortunately, hundreds of languages have fewer than 25 speakers remaining and may soon be lost forever. 30

---

[1] An **anthropologist** is someone who studies people, societies, and culture.

329 words   **Time taken** _____

Reading Comprehension

Choose the correct answers for the following questions.

1 The main idea of this reading is that _____.
   a people should learn new languages
   b languages help us understand other cultures
   c many languages are disappearing around the world
   d most people speak English, Spanish, and Mandarin

2 Why are local languages being spoken less and less?
   a People use computers to communicate now.
   b Children do not talk to their grandparents.
   c People who know the language don't want to speak to each other.
   d People prefer to learn and speak more common languages.

3 When is a language considered to be dying?
   a when about 50 percent of local people speak it
   b when fewer than 30 percent of local children learn it
   c when it doesn't have a dictionary
   d when it is only spoken by old people

4 What does Dr. Cumberland mean when she says *no one language gets it all* in lines 18–19?
   a There are too many different languages.
   b There are many ways to understand the world.
   c Some cultures understand the world the wrong way.
   d We need to look for one language that can explain the world.

5 According to Dr. Cumberland, to save a dying language, you need to _____.
   a understand the culture's history
   b listen to people who still speak it
   c teach all the children who speak it
   d be able to speak English, Spanish, or Mandarin

6 Why was it so hard for linguists to study Ayanpaneco?
   a It's a very difficult language.
   b They couldn't understand the grammar.
   c There were fewer than 25 speakers left.
   d The people who knew the language didn't speak to each other.

Turn to page 176 to record your reading fluency progress. First, find the vertical line that is closest to your reading rate. Next, how many of the six comprehension questions did you answer correctly? Find the point on the graph where your reading rate and your comprehension score meet. Mark that spot with a dot.
Which quadrant does the dot fall in? Your goal is to be a fluent reader and score in quadrant four.

Review Reading 6: Celebrating Chusok

Fluency Practice

Time yourself as you read through the passage. Write your time in the space at the bottom of the page. Then answer the questions on the next page.

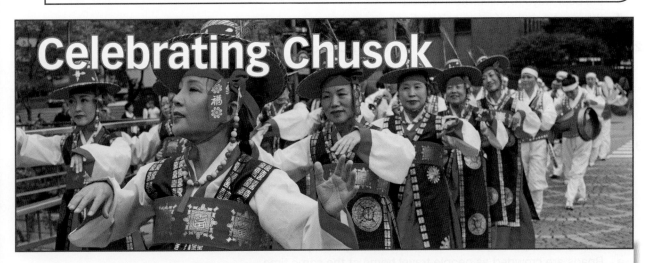

Celebrating Chusok

Chusok is one of the most important festivals in the Korean calendar. It takes place in the eighth month of the lunar calendar (in either September or October), on the night of the full moon. Chusok is a time for family reunions and for people to honor and give thanks to their ancestors. It is also meant to celebrate nature and the large harvest[1] that it has given them.

5 Nowadays, many people in Korea live and work in big cities like Seoul. During Chusok, people who have moved away return to their hometowns in the countryside to celebrate together. The government gives everyone a day off from work before and after Chusok. Many people spend those days traveling, as the roads are very busy during this period. A two-hour journey can easily turn into six hours!

10 At the family home, the day before Chusok is spent cleaning the home and preparing food for ceremonies and family dinners. Women make *songphyun*—moon-shaped rice cakes with a sweet filling—using new rice from the recent harvest. It is said that the woman who makes the most beautiful *songphyun* will find a good-looking husband or give birth to a beautiful daughter. The *songphyun* can take days to make, but now people can buy them easily in stores.

15 The next day is Chusok. People make an effort to dress nicely and wear traditional costumes like the *hanbok*, although this is more common among the older women. In the morning, food is placed on a special table dedicated to their ancestors, and families pay a visit their graves. Later, traditional games like *yut nori* (a game of throwing sticks) and *hwa-tu* (a card game) are played. At night, the whole family goes outdoors under the full moon, and everyone eats and drinks until
20 late. The third day is usually spent traveling back home and preparing to return to work or school.

Like Thanksgiving and Lunar New Year, Chusok is a time for families to reconnect with past traditions, as well as spend time with each other.

---

[1] A **harvest** is the gathering of crops, such as rice, wheat, or potatoes.   **355 words**   **Time taken** _____

Reading Comprehension

Choose the correct answers for the following questions.

1 This reading is mainly about _____ .
   a the ways that Chusok has changed over the years
   b what Chusok is, and how it is celebrated
   c the best ways to celebrate in Korea
   d the most popular Korean celebrations

2 Which of these do people **NOT** celebrate during Chusok?
   a nature
   b a big harvest
   c relatives who have died
   d marriage and babies

3 According to the passage, in what ways has Chusok **NOT** changed?
   a Younger women don't wear the *hanbok* very much.
   b People now eat *songphyun* during Chusok.
   c More people live in big cities.
   d People can now buy *songphyun* in stores.

4 According to the passage, why does a two-hour journey become six hours?
   a Roads are crowded as people travel home at the same time.
   b People stop to visit the graves of their ancestors.
   c People have to buy food for ceremonies.
   d The government closes roads for celebrations.

5 What do people **NOT** do on the day before Chusok?
   a travel
   b play games
   c make *songphyun*
   d clean the house

6 Which of the following is **NOT** part of the Chusok celebrations?
   a making moon-shaped rice cakes
   b dressing in nice clothes
   c going outdoors under the moon
   d greeting family members by saying "Chusok!"

Turn to page 176 to record your reading fluency progress. First, find the vertical line that is closest to your reading rate. Next, how many of the six comprehension questions did you answer correctly? Find the point on the graph where your reading rate and your comprehension score meet. Mark that spot with a dot. Which quadrant does the dot fall in? Your goal is to be a fluent reader and score in quadrant four.

Getting Ready

Discuss the following questions with a partner.

1 What life events are shown in the pictures above? How old should a person be to do each activity?
2 Which of these have you experienced?
3 What other major life events can you think of?

CHAPTER 1 The Age of Adulthood

Before You Read
Are You Old Enough?

A The following words are taken from the passage on the next page. Match each word or phrase with its definition.

1 _____ driver's license   **a** to play games to try to win money
2 _____ gamble   **b** drinks like wine, whisky, and beer
3 _____ nightclub   **c** the army, airforce, and navy
4 _____ alcohol   **d** choose members of government
5 _____ military   **e** a paper or card that allows you to drive
6 _____ vote   **f** a place for late-night drinking and dancing

B What do the items in **A** have in common? Discuss with a partner.

Reading Skill
Predicting

Before we read a passage, we can make predictions about a passage. This can help us understand the passage better. Good readers naturally ask themselves questions about what they are about to read.

A Discuss the following questions with a partner.

1 Look at the title of the passage on the next page. What do you think *The Age of Adulthood* means?
2 Look at the photo of the boy. Why do you think he looks so happy?
3 Now read only the first line of each paragraph. Check (✓) what you think you will read about in the passage.

☐ celebrating birthdays   ☐ how your body changes as you get older
☐ buying your first car   ☐ important ages around the world
☐ getting your first job   ☐ the differences between children and adults
☐ what people do at certain ages   ☐ what it means to be an adult

B Skim the passage to see if your ideas in **A** were correct.

C Read the entire passage carefully. Then answer the questions on page 128.

Personalize your classroom. Most learners do better in an environment that they feel belongs to them. As a class, what can you do to personalize your classroom? Maybe you could put up posters or put up jokes and stories for your class to read? Identify three things that you can do together to make your classroom a better place in which to learn.

The Age of Adulthood

In the United States, 16, 18, and 21 are **significant** ages in a person's life. A person can do new things at each age to show that he or she is **no longer** a child. These are all part of the **transition** to adulthood.

5　After turning 16 in the United States, a person can be **employed**, get a driver's license, and leave home. Many high school students learn to drive and get part-time jobs soon after celebrating their 16th birthday. At 18, people in the United States can vote in government
10　elections and join the military, but they are **prohibited** from going into nightclubs, buying alcohol like beer or wine, or gambling until they are 21.

In many Latin American[1] countries, a young woman's 15th birthday is important. At this age, she is no longer **considered** to be a girl, but a woman. To mark
15　this special day, families with 15-year-old daughters have a celebration called a *quinceañera*. The day begins with the young woman and her family going to church. Later, there is a party to which many guests are invited.

20　In Japan, boys and girls are considered to be adults at the age of 20. At this age, they are **allowed** to vote and drink alcohol. The second Monday in January is a national holiday called Coming-of-Age Day. On this day, 20-year-olds celebrate by first going to a shrine[2] with their families. Later, they listen
25　to speeches[3] given by city and school leaders. After that, many celebrate with family and friends late into the night.

In many countries, celebrations do not stop at adulthood. People like to celebrate what they consider to be important ages such as their 50th or 60th birthdays, or significant events such as the birth of their first child,
30　or their **retirement**.

---

[1] **Latin America** is Central and South America.
[2] A **shrine** is a kind of religious building.
[3] A **speech** is a talk given to a group of people.

Reading Comprehension
Check Your Understanding

A Choose the correct answers for the following questions.

1 The main idea of the passage is _____ .
   a the age of adulthood is too young in some places but too old in others
   b being a young person in Latin America is easier than in Japan or the U.S.
   c there are special ages and celebrations around the world that show a person is becoming an adult

2 Americans are NOT allowed to _____ when they turn 18.
   a drive   b buy alcohol   c join the military

3 According to the passage, which of the following shows you are becoming an adult?
   a voting in an election   b throwing a party   c celebrating your birthday

4 What do *quinceañera* and Coming-of-Age Day have in common?
   a Both are only for young women.
   b City and school leaders are involved.
   c They start the day with a religious ceremony.

B Read the following sentences. Check (✔) true (T) or false (F). If the sentence is false, change it to make it true.

		T	F
1	In the United States, 16th, 18th, and 21st birthdays are special occasions.		
2	In many European countries, a young woman's 15th birthday is important.		
3	The *quinceañera* is only celebrated with the family.		
4	Many people think retirement is a big event in their lives.		

Critical Thinking

C Discuss the following questions with a partner.

1 Do you think age plays a big part in determining if someone is an adult? Why, or why not?
2 What ages are important in your country or culture? Why?

Vocabulary Comprehension
Words in Context

A Complete the following sentences with the best answer. The words in blue are from the passage.

1 The _____ man said he was planning to retire.
   a young   b old

2 A transition is _____ .
   a an ending   b a change

3 The children are only allowed to do something if it's _____ .
   a safe   b dangerous

4 People usually _____ significant events.

   a forget   **b** remember

5 When you employ someone, you have to _____ him.

   a pay   **b** help

6 If you consider something to be true, you _____ it is true.

   a can prove   **b** think

7 If something no longer happens, it _____ .

   a takes more time   **b** has stopped

8 Why would something be prohibited?

   a It's too expensive.   **b** It's not good for you.

B **Complete the following sentences using the words in blue from A. You might have to change the form of the word.**

1 Knives, guns, and even scissors are _____ on airplanes.

2 I think that the _____ from life as a student to working life is very difficult.

3 My father decided to _____ last year. He really loved his job, so he's a little unhappy.

4 I _____ Sally my best friend. She's been a very _____ person in my life.

A **Read the following passage and (circle) all of the *trans-* words that you find.**

Happy Landings for Ernesto!

Last week, life didn't look very good for heart transplant patient Ernesto Medina from Spain. He was told two months ago that he would need the operation if he was to survive. He planned to make the transatlantic journey to a hospital in Chicago. While he was in transit at JFK Airport in New York, he received the news that his new heart had been accidentally transported to another hospital. Ernesto then had to get on a different plane to transport him to the other hospital, where the operation was carried out in time. Ernesto is now recovering from the transplant. His English-speaking wife translated for him as he said, "I feel like a new man—this new heart has transformed my life."

Vocabulary Skill

The Prefix *trans-*

In the passage, you read the word *transition*, a word that uses the prefix *trans-*, which means *across*, *change*, or *move from place to place*. *Trans-* comes at the beginning of many words to form nouns, verbs, adjectives, and adverbs in English.

B **Match each of the *trans-* words from A with a definition below.**

1 during a journey; on the way to a place   *in transit*

2 changed completely   _____

3 take, move, or carry something to a different place   _____

4 across the Atlantic Ocean   _____

5 changed from one language into another   _____

6 to remove an organ from someone's body and place in another person's body   _____

Before You Read
Important Firsts

A Look at this list of important *firsts*. (Circle) any that you have experienced. Add one more to the list in the box.

first:			
car	apartment	child	girlfriend/boyfriend _____
job	English class	pet	airplane trip

B Choose one of your firsts from above and tell a partner about it.

Reading Skill
Making Inferences

When we make inferences, we think about the passage and try to understand more than is written there. When we make inferences, we actively ask questions like *What does this mean?* or *Why did the writer/ author write that?* in order to understand what we read more deeply.

A Scan the passage on the next page to find the words shown in italics below. Read the sentences before and after the words to make inferences about the meaning. Then choose the correct answers.

1 In line 1, *University Express* is probably _____.
   a a website
   b a newspaper
   c a television show

2 Which of the following can NOT be inferred about line 5, *I got it the moment I turned 18*?
   a Miguel really wanted to learn how to drive.
   b Miguel's father wanted him to drive.
   c In Spain, you can drive when you turn 18.

3 In line 14, why were the people *very shy*?
   a They didn't know how to dance.
   b They had very little experience with dating.
   c Marta was worried about her best friend

4 In line 23, Soo-Jin overcame his *fear* of _____.
   a backpacking
   b staying in a hostel
   c talking to new people

B Discuss your answers with a partner. How did you arrive at your answer?

C Read the entire passage carefully. Then answer the questions on page 132.

Set your reading rate goal. As you prepare to read, set a reading rate goal. Use your data from the charts at the end of the book. Based on your previous performance, how many words-per-minute do you think you can read now? Time yourself and practice until you reach your goal.

Firsts in Life

In this month's *University Express*, Lynn Zhou **interviews** students around the world about important firsts in their lives. Read their answers to the question:

What was an important first in life for you?

Miguel: For me, an important first was getting my driver's
5   license. I got it the moment I turned 18! Being able to drive my father's car that summer gave me **freedom**, and made me feel like an adult. For example, I'm from Madrid, and my girlfriend is from a **suburb** about 30 kilometers away. Driving made it easy for me to see her more frequently. Also, I was
10 able to take weekend trips with friends to other cities. I really liked being **independent**.

Marta: I went on my first date soon after my 16th birthday. It was with my best friend's brother. He invited me to a movie, but we didn't talk much. We were both very shy.
15 Two weeks later, I went to a high school dance with him, and we had a great time. After that, we spent most of the summer together, but then he and his family **migrated** to France. I guess you could say he was my first boyfriend.

Soo-Jin: An important first for me was traveling from Korea
20 to Europe. When I was 18, I spent the summer with my cousin backpacking through Europe. It was my first time out of Korea so I was nervous and **reluctant** to talk to people. Luckily I **overcame** my fears and **gradually** started to open up. I learned to be more independent. I made friends with other
25 travelers at the hostels we stayed at, and I keep in touch with many of them even now.

Reading Comprehension
Check Your Understanding

A Choose the best answer for the following questions.

1 Which of the following did Miguel NOT do with a car?
   a He visited his girlfriend more often.
   b He visited other cities on weekends.
   c He drove his dad around in the summer.

2 Where did Marta go on her first date?
   a the cinema
   b the high school dance
   c her best friend's house

3 What first does Soo-Jin talk about?
   a his first time staying in a hostel
   b his first time going out of Korea
   c his first time traveling with his cousin

B Read the following sentences. Check (✔) the person that best matches each sentence.

This person...	Miguel	Marta	Soo-Jin
used to be shy.			
lives in a big city.			
went on a date at the age of 16.			
has friends from around the world.			
talks about being independent.			

Critical Thinking

C Discuss the following questions with a partner.

1 Do you think Miguel, Marta, and Soo-Jin have different or similar personalities? In what ways?
2 Do you think that young people from around the world have the same idea about what are important firsts? Why, or why not?

Vocabulary Comprehension
Definitions

A Match each word from the reading with its definition. The words in blue are from the passage.

1 _____ freedom
2 _____ migrate
3 _____ reluctant
4 _____ gradually
5 _____ independent
6 _____ interview
7 _____ overcome
8 _____ suburb

a the ability to do what you want
b not needing the help of other people
c move to a different country or place
d to deal with and solve a problem
e part of a town or city outside the center
f slowly; little by little
g unwilling to do something
h to ask a person questions to get information

B Complete the following sentences using the correct form of words from **A**.

1 You don't look very friendly, so people are _____ to talk to you.
2 That lucky reporter was given a chance to _____ the president.
3 My family is moving to a nearby _____. I don't want to move; I love the downtown area too much!
4 I've become much more _____ since I started living by myself. My parents _____ to another country last year.

A Look at the list of words below that begin with the prefix *sub-*. Match each word with a definition on the right.

1 _____ submissive
2 _____ subtitles
3 _____ subway
4 _____ submerge
5 _____ subside
6 _____ submarine

a an underwater ship
b to become less, e.g. less strong or loud
c an underground transportation system
d willing to follow or listen to someone without arguing
e to go below the surface of water or another liquid
f words on the bottom of a movie screen that translate the actor's or narrator's words

Vocabulary Skill
The Prefix *sub-*

In this chapter, you learned the word *suburb*. *Sub-* is a prefix that usually means *under, lower,* or *on the outside*. It can come at the beginning of a noun, verb, adjective, or adverb.

B Complete the sentences below using the correct form of the words from **A**.

1 This city has a variety of transportation: electric buses, taxis, monorails, and a _____ system.
2 Scientists have developed a new kind of _____ that can stay in the ocean for one year.
3 He believes that wives should be _____ to their husbands. I definitely don't agree with him!
4 I can't swim well because I don't like _____ my head in water.
5 The doctor told me to take this pill and wait for my headache to _____ .
6 I don't speak French, so I had to read the _____ all the time when watching the French movie.

Real Life Skill
Choosing the Right Word

English has many groups of words that are similar in meaning but are used differently. A good English language dictionary can explain these differences. Usage notes in dictionaries tell you how and when to use a word.

A The following words in red have almost the same meaning but are used in very different ways. Read their meanings and how they are used.

land

1 an area of ground that is not covered by water: *After sailing for a month, the sailors saw* **land**.

2 an area that someone owns as property: *In New York City,* **land** *is very expensive.*

3 a country or nation

ground
floor

Ground means the surface we walk on, but when this is indoors, it is the *floor*: *When we have a picnic, we sit on the* **ground**. *When I watch TV, I sit on the* **floor**.

soil
earth

The substance in which plants grow is *soil* or *earth*. However, **Earth** with a capital E refers to our planet:

The **soil** *in Thailand is good for growing rice. The farmer picked up a handful of* **earth**. *After a month in space, the astronaut returned to* **Earth**.

B Complete the following sentences using *land, ground, floor, soil,* and *Earth.* Discuss your answers with a partner.

1 In some countries, people don't sleep in beds. They feel more comfortable sleeping on the _____.

2 I am considering buying a piece of _____ and building my retirement home.

3 You should put a plastic sheet on the _____ before you sit down, as it just rained.

4 _____ contains many different types of materials, including small pieces of rock, dust, sand, and even living things.

5 Scientists are looking for planets that have the same living conditions as on _____.

6 The ship sailed further out into the ocean until I could no longer see any _____.

What do you think?

1 What firsts do you hope to experience in the future?

2 Imagine you are going to live and work in an English-speaking country. What firsts do you think you will experience?

3 When you celebrate firsts, do you prefer to have a big celebration with lots of people, or just a small party with friends? Explain your reasons.

Look into the Future

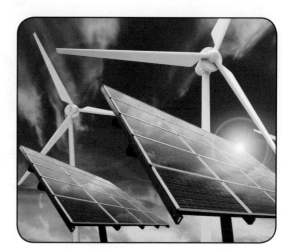

Getting Ready

Discuss the following questions with a partner.

1 Do you believe you are in control of your future? Why, or why not?
2 Have you ever made a prediction about something that would happen in the future? Did your prediction come true?
3 Look at the pictures above. What do you think the world will be like in 50 years' time?

Before You Read
The Zodiac

A Do you know these 12 star signs and what they symbolize? Match the star sign to the correct picture by writing letters in the boxes.

a Aquarius	**b** Aries	**c** Cancer	**d** Capricorn
e Gemini	**f** Leo	**g** Libra	**h** Pisces
i Sagittarius	**j** Scorpio	**k** Taurus	**l** Virgo

B Discuss your answers above with a partner. What is your star sign? What do you know about it?

Reading Skill
Summarizing

When you summarize, you shorten a passage into one or more sentences which describe the main idea. First scan the paragraphs to find the main idea, then combine the most important parts to form a sentence.

A Scan the first paragraph of the passage on the next page. What is the main idea of the paragraph? Discuss your answer with a partner.

B Scan the remaining paragraphs. Match the paragraphs to the main ideas.

1 _____ Paragraph 2   **a** A new sign, Ophiuchus, might be added to the zodiac.

2 _____ Paragraph 3   **b** Many people may find themselves with a different star sign.

3 _____ Paragraph 4   **c** Astrologers used the positions of stars to decide the zodiac.

4 _____ Paragraph 5   **d** Some believe the zodiac determines your personality and future.

C Now read the entire passage carefully. Then answer the questions on page 138.

Are You an Ophiuchus?

1 Thousands of years ago, the **ancient** people of Babylon and Egypt studied the stars in the sky. From their research, they **came up with** the zodiac, a map of the
5 sun, moon, stars, and planets. It was first used to **keep track of** time.

2 These ancient astrologers studied the constellations[1] and their positions in the sky. They wanted to know when each
10 constellation was closest to the sun. They used this information to determine where each group of stars belongs in the zodiac. The word *zodiac* actually means "circle of little animals" in Latin, and refers to how
15 the constellations are shaped.

3 Today, some people believe that the zodiac can be used to describe a person's personality. Some also believe that by studying the zodiac, they can predict what will happen in the future. According to these beliefs, a person's zodiac sign is **connected** to his or her birth date.

4 20 The zodiac has remained the same for over a thousand years. It is **broken up** into 12 equal parts, each **associated** with a star sign. However, some astrologers are suggesting a change—they think a thirteenth sign should be added to the zodiac calendar. This is because the way the Earth rotates has changed slightly over the centuries, which has also changed its path around the sun. This possible thirteenth
25 sign is a constellation called Ophiuchus (pronounced *of-ee-yoo-kuhs*), which means holder of the snake. Ophiuchus is close to the sun from November 29 to December 17.

5 If the dates of the other 12 signs were **adjusted** to make Ophiuchus a sign, many people would have a different star sign. As this new sign falls between Scorpio and Sagittarius, some people with those star signs would have to **switch** to being
30 Ophiuchus. And this would have an effect on dates of the other star signs as well. This would add a whole new answer to the question, "What's your sign?"

[1] A **constellation** is a pattern made by stars in the sky.

Reading Comprehension
Check Your Understanding

A **Choose the correct answers for the following questions.**

1 The zodiac was first invented to _____.
   a predict the future   **b** study the stars   **c** keep track of time

2 Some people believe a person's zodiac sign can tell us about his or her _____.
   a personality   **b** birth date   **c** family background

3 The zodiac is determined by the position of the _____ to the _____.
   a constellations, moon   **b** constellations, sun   **c** Earth, sun

4 If Ophiuchus is made a star sign, many people will _____.
   a have a different birthday
   b have a different star sign
   c stop believing in the zodiac

B **Read the sentences below. Check (✔) true (T) or false (F). If the sentence is false, change it to make it true.**

		T	F
1	Ancient people were very interested in the stars.		
2	If Ophiuchus is made a sign, it will replace Scorpio.		
3	Ophiuchus means "holder of the snake."		
4	All astrologers agree that there should be 13 zodiac signs.		

Critical Thinking

C **Discuss the following questions with your partner.**

1 Why do you think people still believe in the zodiac?

2 What other connections do you think people might make between their lives and the Earth or sky?

Vocabulary Comprehension
Odd Word Out

A **For each group, (circle) the word or phrase that does not belong. The words in blue are from the passage.**

1	came up with	think of	forget
2	put together	connect	keep apart
3	switch	stay the same	exchange
4	measure	adjust	weigh
5	keep track of	remember	ignore
6	unite	break up into	take apart
7	associate	connect	divide
8	ancient	brand new	recent

B **Complete the following sentences using words in blue from A.**

1 Countries are usually _____ smaller parts called states or provinces.

2 I'll have to _____ from coffee to juice because coffee is keeping me awake at night.

3 Email helps me stay _____ with my friends, so I can _____ what's happening in their lives.

4 We usually _____ good ideas when we work as a team.

A **Match each phrasal verb with its meaning. Use your dictionary to help you.**

1 _____ act up   **a** to be with friends, to relax

2 _____ come up with   **b** to stretch before exercising

3 _____ drop in   **c** begin to work

4 _____ hang out   **d** to think of an idea

5 _____ kick in   **e** to die

6 _____ warm up   **f** to get rid of (a sickness), get better

7 _____ pass away   **g** to visit unexpectedly

8 _____ shake off   **h** to behave badly, like a child

B **Complete the following sentences using the correct form of phrasal verbs from A.**

1 Before every game, my teammates and I _____ by running laps and stretching.

2 Danny is always getting in trouble because he always _____ in class.

3 It's impossible to _____ birthday gift ideas for my mother. She's hard to buy gifts for.

4 Let's _____ at the pool today. It's too hot to play baseball.

5 After you finish your sixth month with the company, your health insurance will _____.

6 Karen's house is on the way back. Let's _____ to say hi.

7 It might take a week to _____ your cold. Until then, drink lots of water and rest.

8 Paul is sad because his grandmother _____ last week.

Vocabulary Skill
Phrasal Verbs

A phrasal verb is a special kind of verb made up of a verb and a preposition. Phrasal verbs can be confusing, because their meanings are different from the original verb's meaning. The best way to learn the meaning of a phrasal verb is to use a dictionary.

Try it again! Try reading the passage again to see if you can read it more fluently. Reading a passage up to three times before answering the comprehension questions will help you improve your reading fluency.

Before You Read
Predicting an Earthquake

Major earthquakes happen, on average, only about once per year, but thousands of very small earthquakes happen every day all over the world. The areas marked in red are places where there are the most earthquakes.

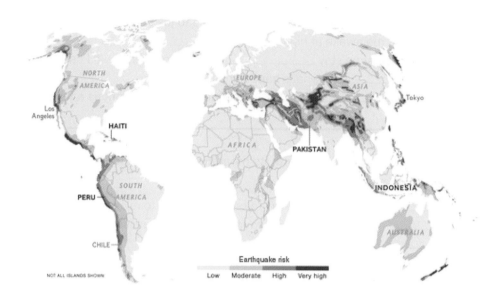

A **Think about answers to the following questions.**

1 Look at the map above. Where do most earthquakes happen? Why do you think they happen in these places?
2 Have you ever experienced an earthquake? What did you feel or see?

B **Discuss your answers with a partner.**

Reading Skill
Identifying Transition Words

Transition words make connections between ideas clear. When we recognize and understand them, our reading comprehension and speed increase.

A Scan the passage on the next page. Circle the following transition words or phrases that appear in the passage.

a however	**b** furthermore	**c** on the other hand	**d** also
e in short	**f** in fact	**g** but	**h** since

B What is the meaning of the transition words/phrases in A? Write the letter of each word next to their meaning. Some may have more than one meaning.

1 _____ to show that something is different
2 _____ to summarize
3 _____ to add information
4 _____ to give details
5 _____ to show a reason

C Now read the entire passage carefully. Then answer the questions on page 142.

Can Animals Predict Earthquakes?

Dear Scientist Sam,

I noticed my dog acting very nervous only a few minutes before a **recent** earthquake shook the house. Is it possible that my dog knew the earthquake was going to happen?

Janet

Sam's reply:

Well, Janet, people have believed for many centuries that animals can predict earthquakes. In fact, we can look back to records from the ancient Greeks. They noticed that animals acted **oddly** in the hours before earthquakes. Even now, people talk about dogs that won't stop barking and cats that won't come out of hiding before an earthquake. Furthermore, strange behavior like this before earthquakes isn't **limited** to pets. People have also reported seeing chickens stop laying eggs, bees leaving their homes, and big groups of fish dying mysteriously in the hours before a natural disaster hits.

It's hard to answer your question, since not all seismologists[1] or animal experts agree that animals can predict earthquakes. Those that disagree **claim** that we should **take into account** other things that affect animal behavior, such as hunger. On the other hand, many people who believe that animals can predict earthquakes often have records of very strange animal behavior right before the ground shakes. To them, this is **evidence** that animals can indeed predict earthquakes.

In short, the **truth** is that we aren't sure. Animals might be able to **sense** earthquakes before they happen, but there is no solid evidence that they can. However, one thing that most seismologists can agree on is that more research is needed. Animals may be the key to predicting earthquakes before they happen, and could help save many lives.

[1] A **seismologist** is a scientist who studies earthquakes and movements of the earth.

Reading Comprehension
Check Your Understanding

A **Choose the correct answers for the following questions.**

1 Janet wrote to Scientist Sam to find out _____.
   a how and why earthquakes happen
   b the history of animals and earthquakes
   c if animals can predict earthquakes

2 According to the passage, which of these statements is correct?
   a People have always believed that animals can predict earthquakes.
   b People believe that animals can be trained to predict earthquakes.
   c People have only recently believed animals can predict earthquakes.

3 Which of these is NOT a reason that Scientist Sam cannot really answer Janet's question?
   a People have different opinions on the issue.
   b He personally does not believe animals can predict earthquakes.
   c There is not enough evidence to prove anything.

4 Seismologists all agree that _____.
   a animals cannot predict earthquakes
   b there is not enough research on this topic
   c we can understand earthquakes by researching animals

B **Read the sentences below. Check (✔) true (T), false (F), or not given (NG). If the sentence is false, change it to make it true.**

		T	F	NG
1	Earthquakes are easy to predict.			
2	The ancient Greeks had cats and dogs for pets.			
3	People say animals can act strangely for other reasons.			
4	There is a new study to prove animals can predict earthquakes.			

Critical Thinking

C **Discuss the following questions with a partner.**

1 Do you think it's possible to predict when and where an earthquake will happen? Why, or why not?

2 Do you believe that animals can detect things that humans can't? Why, or why not?

Vocabulary Comprehension
Words in Context

A **Complete each sentence with the best answer. The words in blue are from the passage.**

1 One example of evidence is _____.
   a fingerprints   b intelligence

2 If someone claims something is true, then the information is _____.
   a possibly true   b proven to be true

3   When you have a limited amount of something, there _____.
    a   will be extra for later   b   might not be enough
4   If you take something into account, you _____ it.
    a   forget about   b   consider
5   Kate always tells the truth, so you should _____ her story.
    a   believe   b   not believe
6   When you sense something, you _____.
    a   are aware of it   b   see it
7   When something seems odd, it is _____.
    a   strange   b   normal
8   If something happened recently, it might have happened _____.
    a   many years ago   b   a few days ago

B   Complete the following sentences with the words in blue from A. You might have to change the form of the word.

1   Not everyone will be able to join the lecture since space is _____.
2   The police need to collect _____ from the crime scene.
3   The man was walking really close to him, so it was _____ that
    he didn't _____ any danger.
4   Chris _____ he was late for work because he didn't
    _____ the bad traffic.

A   Add the suffix -ness to the adjectives in the box to form nouns. Use the nouns to complete the sentences below.

> shy   kind   happy   dark   useful   weak

1   There is a common saying that money doesn't buy you _____.
2   Mother Theresa's _____ was clear in the way she cared for
    thousands of street people.
3   I wish I could stick to a healthy diet, but I have a _____ for
    chocolates.
4   The entire street is in _____ because the electricity was cut off.
5   My brother gets really nervous when a pretty girl talks to him. He can't
    seem to overcome his _____.
6   Before I moved overseas, I wasn't sure about the _____ of
    learning another language.

B   Write the noun form of each of the adjectives below. Not all of them use the suffix -ness. Use your dictionary to help you.

1   formal   _____   2   forgetful   _____   3   convenient   _____
4   valuable   _____   5   curious   _____   6   open   _____
7   flashy   _____   8   loud   _____

Vocabulary Skill
The Suffixes -ness

The suffix -ness is used to change certain adjectives into nouns. When we add the suffix -ness to the adjective *strange*, the adjective becomes the noun *strangeness*. For adjectives of more than one syllable that end in -y, change y to i before adding -ness.

Real Life Skill
Doing Research on the Internet

Searching the Internet is an important skill. Even if you can't understand all the words on a website, your scanning skills can guide you to the information you want.

A **Read the following paragraph about predicting the weather.**

Meteorologists, scientists that study weather patterns, often use high-tech instruments to predict the weather. But people have been making weather forecasts long before these instruments and methods were invented. They usually based their predictions on what they observed in the sky or the way animals behaved. They passed down their knowledge by making it into sayings that are easy for people to remember. These are called proverbs.

B **Read the following weather proverbs, then discuss their meanings with a partner.**

When sea-gulls fly to land, a storm is at hand.

Red sky at night, sailor's delight. Red sky in the morning, sailor take warning.

The higher the clouds the better the weather.

When the night goes to bed with a fever, it will awake with a wet head.

When the forest murmurs and the mountain roars, then close your windows and shut your doors.

C **Do an Internet search and find the meaning of the proverbs. Were you correct?**

D **Now do an Internet search to find a few proverbs on one of the following topics. Explain their meanings to your partner.**

food   friendship   health   money

What do you think?

1 Would you like to know what happens in your future? Why, or why not?
2 Do you know of any books or movies that are set in the future? What was the future like?
3 Where do you see yourself in 10, 20, and 50 years' time?

The Power of Stories UNIT 12

Getting Ready

A The pictures above are scenes from famous folktales. What is happening in each scene?

B Match the picture to the correct folktale below.

a Hansel and Gretel	**c** The Pied Piper of Hamelin
b Little Red Riding Hood	

C Discuss your answers with a partner. Do you know of any folktales from your country or culture?

Before You Read
Special Foods and Drinks

A Ginger buds are the parts of the ginger plant that develop into flowers. They are said to make a person forgetful if eaten. Have you heard of other foods that affect how you feel?

Foods and drinks that . . .	Examples
give you nightmares	
make you sleepy	
wake you up	
make you smarter	
make you happy	

B Compare your answers with a partner.

Reading Skill
Recognizing Sequence of Events

Some passages are organized according to a sequence of events. Words such as *first*, *then*, or *after* can help us to know the order of events.

A These events are from the story on the next page. Without reading the passage, number them in the correct order.

a ____ "Delicious!" declared the rich man loudly.

b ____ The next morning, the innkeeper said goodbye to the rich man.

c ____ One day, a rich man stopped at an inn.

d ____ Later that evening, the rich man came down the stairs and requested dinner.

e ____ The rich man requested the most luxurious room at the inn.

f ____ Then he went upstairs to dress for dinner.

g ____ After he finished his dinner, he went to bed happy, full of ginger buds.

h ____ The innkeeper served him dish after dish of ginger buds.

B Circle any words in the sentences that helped you choose the correct order. Then compare your answers with a partner.

C Quickly skim the story. Compare the events in the passage with the order of events in your time line above.

D Read the entire passage carefully. Then answer the questions on page 148.

Evaluate your progress. Use the reading rate and reading comprehension charts at the end of the book to evaluate your progress as a reader. In what ways are you better today than you were earlier in this course? What things do you still need to work on to become a better reader?

A Japanese Folktale

Once upon a time, in a Japanese mountain inn,[1] there was a **greedy** innkeeper[2] who was always thinking about money.

One day, a rich man stopped at the inn. The innkeeper looked at the guest's fat money belt and thought, "Oh, if only all that money could be mine!" The rich
5 man **requested** the most **luxurious** room at the inn. Then he went up to his room to dress for dinner.

Now, all around the inn there grew **delicate** Japanese ginger plants. In Japan, there is a saying that eating too many ginger buds makes you stupid and forgetful. This gave the innkeeper an idea.

10 "This evening for dinner I'll serve ginger bud tempura!"[3] she thought. "Then, when the rich man leaves in the morning, he'll be forgetful and leave his money belt behind!" She
15 ran into the kitchen and started cooking up the most delicious ginger bud tempura she had ever made.

Later that evening, the rich man
20 came down the stairs and requested dinner. The innkeeper could hardly contain her **delight** as she served him **dish** after dish of ginger buds. "Delicious!" **declared** the rich man loudly. After he finished his dinner, he went to bed happy, full of ginger buds.

The next morning, the innkeeper said goodbye to the rich man. As soon as he
25 was out of sight, she raced up to his room. She looked all over the room for the money belt, but she couldn't find it. Suddenly, she noticed a piece of paper on the floor. It was the rich man's bill. He had forgotten to pay it! She ran after him, down the stairs, out the front door, and up the road until she was **out of breath**, but the rich man was already far, far away.

[1] An **inn** is a small, country-style hotel.
[2] An **innkeeper** is the manager of an inn.
[3] **Tempura** is a style of Japanese cooking.

Reading Comprehension
Check Your Understanding

A **Choose the best answer for the following questions.**

1 What lesson does the author want us to learn from this story?
   a Innkeepers are always thinking about money.
   b Trying to take things that belong to others is wrong.
   c If you ever stay at a country inn, be careful about your money.

2 After the rich man left, the innkeeper raced up to the room to
   _____.
   a check if he paid his bill
   b look for his money belt
   c clean the room

3 After he left the inn, the rich man was probably _____.
   a very angry at the innkeeper
   b feeling lucky that he didn't lose his money
   c not aware that anything had happened

4 Who ended up losing in the end?
   a the innkeeper
   b the rich man
   c both of them

B **Read the following sentences. Check (✔) true (T) or false (F). If the sentence is false, change it to make it true.**

		T	F
1	The rich man stayed at the inn because he wanted ginger bud tempura.		
2	The rich man changed his clothes before dinner.		
3	The rich man knew that the innkeeper wanted his money belt.		
4	The innkeeper ran after the rich man because he had taken her money.		

Critical Thinking

C **Discuss the following questions with a partner.**

1 What is the moral or lesson of the story? Do you think the innkeeper deserved it?

2 Is this story realistic? Do you think greedy people get what they deserve?

Vocabulary Comprehension
Odd Word Out

A **For each group, circle the word or phrase that does not belong. The words in blue are from the passage.**

1	delicate	rough	strong
2	tired	out of breath	frightened
3	delight	disapproval	excitement
4	plate	dish	flag

5	independent	free	greedy
6	request	deserve	ask
7	expensive	luxurious	plain
8	announce	deny	declare

B Complete the following sentences using the words in blue from **A**.
You might have to change the form of the word.

1   Leila is _____ because she ran all the way home.
2   The government _____ that next Friday will be a national holiday.
3   Please take care when moving that painting. It's very _____.
4   You could see the _____ on the _____ man's
    face when he was given some money.

A   **Look at some examples of how adverbs are formed.**

Many adverbs are formed by adding -*ly* to the end of an adjective.

> *The dog made a sudden movement.*   *The dog moved suddenly.*

When adjectives end in -*le*, we change the *e* to a *y*.

> *This chair is very comfortable.*   *Are you sitting comfortably?*

When adjectives end in -*y*, we change the *y* to an *i* and add -*ly*.

> *The greedy woman looked at the*   *The woman looked greedily*
> *money belt.*   *at the money belt.*

B   **Write the adverb form of these adjectives.**

Adjective		Adverb	Adjective		Adverb
1	crazy		5	fierce	
2	legal		6	curious	
3	natural		7	nice	
4	delicate		8	hungry	

C   **Complete the following sentences using the words from B.**

1   The dog barked _____ at the robbers.
2   For 16-year-olds, drinking alcohol is _____ prohibited.
3   Children are _____ very _____ about the world around them.
4   If you ask him _____ , he might decide to help you.
5   He hadn't eaten all day, so he stared at the food _____.
6   You must be _____ if you think you can get into the concert without a ticket.

Vocabulary Skill
Adverbs

> The words *loudly* and
> *suddenly* appeared in
> *A Japanese Folktale*.
> These are examples
> of adverbs. Adverbs
> can be used to
> describe verbs in a
> sentence; they tell us
> the manner or way in
> which something is
> done.

Before You Read
Believe It or Not!

A A hoax is something created to trick or deceive people. Read the following sentences. Check (✔) if you think they are true stories (T) or hoaxes (H).

		T	H
1	A man in Canada owned a cat that weighed 40 kilograms.		
2	There is a Dog Island where 2,500 dogs live in freedom without owners.		
3	A monkey named Marty can type fluently in English.		
4	There is a website that can send food smells to your computer through the Internet.		
5	Some people have found a way to charge your cell phone using just an onion and a sports drink.		

B Compare your answers with a partner. The answers are at the bottom on the next page.

Reading Skill
Identifying Cause and Effect

> One relationship between two ideas in a text is *cause and effect.* In the text, the cause can come before or after the effect. Using the word *because* in a sentence can help show the cause. The idea that follows *because* is the cause; for example, I can't sleep (effect) because I drank too much coffee (cause).

A Read the following pairs of sentences which relate to the passage on the next page. Which is the cause and which is the effect? Write *C* or *E*.

Paragraph 2

1 _____ The airline ran a special promotion.
  _____ Many people visited the airline's website.

2 _____ Airfare is expensive.
  _____ People asked the airline for discounts.

Paragraph 3

3 _____ There was a hurricane.
  _____ New Orleans was flooded.

4 _____ People were afraid.
  _____ A photo of a giant crocodile was sent around the Internet.

Paragraph 4

5 _____ People send the chain email to their friends.
  _____ People believe they might make money.

6 _____ The sender claims he thought it was a lie, but it was actually true.
  _____ More people believe the email.

B Scan the passage to find the causes and effects mentioned above. Were your answers correct?

C Now read the entire passage carefully. Then answer the questions on page 152.

INTERNET HOAXES

1 The Internet is a fast and convenient way of sending and **obtaining** information, but it's also a very easy way to spread misinformation. And new **hoaxes** pop up almost every day about anything from **shocking** celebrity deaths to mystery objects in foods. Here are three examples of Internet hoaxes.

2
Pay what you weigh
5 On April 1, 2011, New Zealand Air began advertising a one-day **fare** sale—pay what you weigh. The airline's website offered visitors a chance to pay a dollar amount that was equal to their weight in kilograms. The idea was "more weight = more fuel = more cost" and many people believed it. The **promotion** brought
10 thousands of visitors to the company's website and became a popular news story. In the end, though, the promotion turned out to be an April Fool's[1] joke.

3
Croc on the loose
While the streets of New Orleans were still flooded after a **terrible**
15 hurricane, a frightening email was sent around the Internet. It included a photograph of an **immense** crocodile over five meters long. According to the
20 message, it had been swimming around the flooded city eating people. It was later discovered that the photographs of the crocodile were of one that was
25 caught in the Congo[2] years before.

4
Earn money through emails
The following email hoax **fooled** many people. The sender claims that a large company will pay you to send their email to as many people as possible. For every person that you send the email to, the company promises you will
30 receive $5; for every person that person sends it to, you'll get $3; and for every third person those people send it to, you will be paid $1. To make the lie even more believable, the sender says that at first he thought it was a hoax, but the company soon sent him $800.

---

[1] **April Fool's Day** is celebrated as a day when people play tricks and hoaxes on each other.
[2] **The Congo** is an area in Africa.

Answers to Before You Read—: They are all Internet hoaxes.

Reading Comprehension
Check Your Understanding

A **Choose the correct answers for the following questions.**

1 The purpose of this passage is to _____.
  a tell people to be careful of Internet hoaxes
  b show how anyone can create an Internet hoax
  c explain that, even though they seem false, Internet hoaxes might be true

2 The New Zealand Air hoax was based on _____.
  a free vacations   b the weather   c peoples' weight

3 The crocodile in the photograph was from _____.
  a New Orleans   b New Zealand   c the Congo

4 Some people believed they could make money by _____.
  a sending emails   b receiving emails   c reading emails

B **Read the following sentences. Check (✔) true (T) or false (F). If the sentence is false, change it to make it true.**

According to the passage,...	T	F
1 people could save money on flights if their weight was less than the cost of a ticket.		
2 the city of New Orleans was really flooded.		
3 a huge crocodile ate several people in New Orleans.		
4 someone really received $800 for sending emails.		

Critical Thinking

C **Discuss the following questions with a partner.**

1 Do you think the New Zealand Air hoax was mean? Why, or why not?
2 How can you tell if a story or an email offer is a hoax?

Vocabulary Comprehension
Definitions

A **Match each word with its definition. The words in blue are from the passage.**

1 _____ obtain   a the price for a ride on something
2 _____ fare   b very bad
3 _____ immense   c to trick or deceive someone
4 _____ hoax   d a piece of false information meant to trick people
5 _____ shock   e special advertising to help sell something
6 _____ terrible   f to get something
7 _____ fool   g very big
8 _____ promotion   h something that is unpleasant, upsetting, or very surprising

B Complete the following sentences using the words in blue from **A**. You might have to change the form of the word.

1 The man _____ many people into giving him money by pretending he needed it for his bus _____ home.

2 He must have _____ my password in order to get into my email account.

3 There was a(n) _____ thunderstorm after a week of no rain.

4 There's a _____ at the store where you can buy two shampoos for the price of one.

A Look at this list of nouns that are also verbs. Can you add any more to the list?

water	mask	compliment	_____
mail	host	light	_____
stamp	salt	phone	_____
cover	support	vote	_____

B Complete the following sentences by replacing the phrase in parentheses with the correct form of the verbs from **A**.

1 Martha, will you please (*pour water on*) _____ the plants during my vacation?

2 Stan is always (*giving compliments to*) _____ Leslie. I think he likes her.

3 If you're going to be late, you should (*make a phone call to*) _____ the restaurant.

4 Please consider (*casting your vote*) _____ for Sue Whitford for president.

5 Mel (*was the host at*) _____ a really big party last night. It was a nice chance for new students to socialize.

6 During the winter, my father (*puts a cover on*) _____ our swimming pool.

7 Although we didn't have a flashlight, the moon (*shined light on*) _____ our way to the beach.

8 I've already (*put salt in*) _____ the soup, so you don't need to add any more.

Vocabulary Skill
Nouns That Are Also Verbs

Over time, some nouns become verbs in English. This process is called *verbing*. Some of the older products of *verbing* are *salt* and *mail*, while newer ones are *blog* and *gift*.

Celebrate your achievements. As a class, did you achieve your goal of becoming fluent readers? Fluent readers read at 200 wpm with 70 percent comprehension. As a class, did you achieve this goal? If so, celebrate your achievement together!

Real Life Skill

Understanding Internet Speak

Many English words have taken on a different meaning when used in relation to the Internet. For example, the search engine Google is so popular that people have started saying *google* in place of the word search. Some words or phrases are also more commonly expressed as abbreviations in chat rooms and emails in order to save time; for example, *FYI (for your information)*.

A Match these Internet abbreviations with their meanings.

	Abbreviations		Meanings
1	_____ ASAP	a	no problem
2	_____ BTW	b	boyfriend
3	_____ OIC	c	away from keyboard
4	_____ IMO	d	as soon as possible
5	_____ AFK	e	laughs out loud
6	_____ LOL	f	in my opinion
7	_____ NP	g	girlfriend
8	_____ TTYL	h	oh, I see
9	_____ G/F	i	talk to you later
10	_____ B/F	j	by the way

B Look at this list of words that are commonly used on the Internet. With a partner, discuss what the words mean and write them below.

Word	Meaning
app	
friend	
like	
post	
profile	
spam	
tag	
tweet	
virus	

C Email Challenge: Send a partner an email. Use any of the abbreviations and words above, or others that you know.

What do you think?

1 Can you think of any similarities between folktales that you know? What do you think makes a good folktale?

2 Can you think of other examples of famous hoaxes? Why do you think people like to create hoaxes?

3 Do you think there should be punishment for people who create Internet hoaxes? Why or why not, and in which cases?

Fluency Strategy: Reading ACTIVEly

In order to become a more fluent reader, remember to follow the six points of the ACTIVE approach—before, while, and after you read. Turn to the inside front cover for more information on the ACTIVE approach.

Activate Prior Knowledge

Before you read, it's important to think about what you already know about the topic, and what you want to get out of the text.

A Look at the article on the next page. Read only the title and look at the picture. What do you think the article is about? What kinds of things do you think people can be too young for?

B Now read the first sentence of the article. What do you know about this topic? In your country, at what ages can a person drink alcohol or get married? Do you agree with these laws? Discuss with a partner.

Cultivate Vocabulary

As you read, you may come across unknown words. Remember, you don't need to understand all the words in a passage to understand the meaning of the whole passage. Skip the unknown words for now, or guess at their meaning and come back to them later. Note useful new vocabulary in your vocabulary notebook—see page 6 for more advice on vocabulary.

A Now read the first paragraph of the passage. Circle any words or phrases you don't know. Can you understand the rest of the paragraph even if you don't understand those items?

B Write the unknown words here. Without using a dictionary, try to guess their meaning. Use the words around the unknown word and any prefixes, suffixes, or word roots to help you.

New word/phrase	Meaning

Think About Meaning

As you read, think about what you can infer, or *read between the lines*. Think about the author's intentions, attitudes, and purpose for writing.
Read the opening paragraph again and discuss these questions with a partner.
* Do you think this article was written by an old or young person? Where do you think the person lives?
* Why do you think this writer wrote the article? Where might you find this piece of writing?
* What do you think the author means by *should be changed*? Do you think the age should be lowered or raised?

Increase Reading Fluency

To increase your reading fluency, it's important to monitor your own reading habits as you read. Look again at the tips on page 8. As you read, follow those tips.

Now read the whole passage *Young People Are Adults, Too!* As you read, check your predictions from *Think About Meaning* on page 155.

Young People Are Adults, Too!

All around the world, there are laws regarding ages where we can or cannot do things. Many countries, like the United States, have minimum ages for drinking alcohol, driving, gambling, and marriage. I disagree with many of these laws and feel they should be changed. Not because I think children should be allowed to do these things, but because many of these laws concerning young
5   people's freedom don't make sense. I also think they are too inconsistent—they really differ from place to place—especially in the U.S.!

In many U.S. states, the legal age for drinking alcohol is 21, since it's seen as the age where young people become adults. But I feel that most of us are already adults by the time we reach 18—after all, that's when we start college and move out of our family homes. Eighteen is also the age when
10   we can get married. Personally, I think they got it the wrong way round! Why are we allowed to get married at 18, but not allowed to drink alcohol? People should wait until after college to get married, since it's a big decision that affects the rest of our lives.

The legal ages for driving and gambling don't make sense to me either because they are different from place to place. For example, in some states, the driving age is 16, but in others, it is 15.
15   In Hawaii, young people will have to wait until they turn 18 before they can take driving lessons. Gambling is the same. In cities like Colorado, you can only gamble when you turn 21, but you only need to be 18 in New York or 16 in Maine. It's confusing! I wish there weren't so many different laws.

However, there are some laws that are becoming better. For instance, the legal voting age in the U.S. used to be 21, but now it's 18. I hope it'll gradually be made even lower. Young people shouldn't be
20   prohibited from choosing their leaders. I think anyone who wants to vote should be allowed to.

Finally, I think us young people have the power to change this situation. Write to your leaders in the government and let them know how you feel!

Verify Strategies

To build your reading fluency, it's important to be aware of how you use strategies to read, and to consider how successfully you are using them.

Use the questions in the Self Check on the next page to think about your use of reading strategies.

Evaluate Progress

Evaluating your progress means thinking about how much you understood from the passage, and how fluently you were able to read the passage to get the information you needed.

Choose the correct answer for the following questions.

1 The purpose of this passage is to _____.
   a argue for why some minimum age laws should be changed
   b show that the U.S. does not have good laws
   c tell young people when they are able to do things
   d show how young people can work to change laws

2 Why does the writer think that the legal drinking age should be 18?
   a A person is an adult at that age.
   b The writer is going to turn 18 soon.
   c Young people are mature at a younger age now.
   d Young people usually drink in college.

3 What are you NOT allowed to do when you turn 18 in New York?
   a vote
   b get married
   c drink alcohol
   d gamble

4 Which is NOT a reason the writer thinks many laws should be changed?
   a They are different from place to place.
   b They determine adulthood at the wrong age.
   c They do not allow young people to vote.
   d They prohibit young people from doing what they want.

5 Which statement would the writer probably agree with?
   a The minimum age for voting should stay at 18 years old.
   b People should be allowed to drive at a young age.
   c Marriage is a bigger decision to make than drinking alcohol.
   d Young people should not follow laws they do not agree with.

6 How does the writer suggest making changes?
   a by writing letters to government leaders
   b by traveling to another state
   c by writing a blog
   d by breaking the laws

SELF CHECK

A Here is a list of all the reading skills in *Active Skills for Reading Book 1*. For each skill, say whether you found the skill useful, not useful, or if you need more work with it. Check (✓) one of the boxes for each reading skill.

Reading skill	Useful	Not useful	I need work
Distinguishing Main Idea and Supporting Details			
Identifying Cause and Effect			
Identifying Main Ideas			
Identifying Supporting Details			
Identifying Transition Words			
Making Inferences			
Predicting			
Reading for Details			
Recognizing Sequence of Events			
Summarizing			
Scanning			
Skimming for Main Ideas			
Using Subheadings to Predict Content			

B Here are the four fluency strategies covered in the Review Units. For each strategy, say whether you found it useful, not useful, or if you need more work with it. Check (✓) one of the boxes.

Fluency strategy	Useful	Not useful	I need work
SQ3R			
KWL			
Dealing with Unknown Words			
Reading ACTIVEly			

C Look again at the *Are You an Active Reader?* quiz on page 10 and complete the chart again. How has your reading fluency improved since you started this course?

Review Reading 7: The Mystery of the Fortune Cookie

The Mystery of the Fortune Cookie

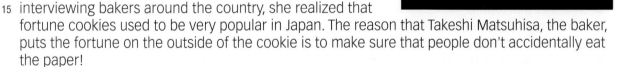

To many people, particularly in America, every good Chinese meal should end with a fortune cookie. So would you believe that one place you won't see a fortune cookie is China?

These cookies have a long and mysterious history—one
5 that doesn't begin in China. According to researcher Yasuko Nakamachi, fortune cookies actually originated in Japan! Ms. Nakamachi first saw Japanese fortune cookies at a bakery while visiting a popular temple outside Kyoto in the 1990s. However, the baker was folding a paper fortune into
10 a fold on the *outside* of the cookie, not the inside, like the fortune cookies we are used to.

Ms. Nakamachi was very curious about this, and decided to do her own research. After spending six years going through thousands of old documents and drawings, and
15 interviewing bakers around the country, she realized that fortune cookies used to be very popular in Japan. The reason that Takeshi Matsuhisa, the baker, puts the fortune on the outside of the cookie is to make sure that people don't accidentally eat the paper!

Ms. Nakamachi found a drawing that went as far back as 1878, showing a Japanese man making
20 the same kind of cookies as Matsuhisa's bakery. This is interesting because a number of people claimed to have invented fortune cookies in California in the 1920s.

If these cookies are a Japanese invention, then why are they served in American Chinese restaurants? After interviewing many Japanese and Chinese American families, Ms. Nakamachi suggested that it's likely that Japanese people first started serving fortune cookies in their
25 restaurants when they moved to the United States. Then Chinese restaurant owners borrowed the idea and began making their own fortune cookies, beginning the now-traditional practice of serving fortune cookies at the end of each meal.

Today, about three billion of these cookies are made annually in the U.S., and are served in restaurants all over the world. Although fortune cookies might not be a traditional snack in
30 China, they have become one for people in many other countries.

345 words   **Time taken** _____

Reading Comprehension

Choose the correct answers for the following questions.

1 This passage is mainly about _____ .
  a how fortune cookies became popular
  b how and where fortune cookies began
  c why Chinese people make fortune cookies
  d how fortune cookies can predict the future

2 Where are fortune cookies usually served and eaten?
  a at Japanese temples
  b in Japanese restaurants in the U.S.
  c in Chinese restaurants in Asia
  d in Chinese restaurants in the U.S.

3 Who is Yasuko Nakamachi?
  a an artist
  b a baker
  c a researcher
  d a restaurant owner

4 What is unique about Takeshi Matsuhisa's cookies?
  a The notes inside give advice.
  b The paper inside tastes delicious.
  c The fortunes are folded on the outside.
  d They are made at a factory in California.

5 What is important about Ms. Nakamichi's discovery of the 1878 drawing?
  a It shows that fortune cookies were popular in Japan and California.
  b It proves that Matsuhisa's bakery was the first to make fortune cookies.
  c It shows that people wanted to draw and write about fortune cookies.
  d It proves that fortune cookies were first made in Japan, not California.

6 Which of these statements is NOT true?
  a Fortune cookies are popular in the U.S.
  b In Japan, the fortunes are put on the outside of the cookie.
  c Fortune cookies were brought to the U.S. by the Chinese.
  d American cookie makers made the fortune cookie popular.

Turn to page 176 to record your reading fluency progress. First, find the vertical line that is closest to your reading rate. Next, how many of the six comprehension questions did you answer correctly? Find the point on the graph where your reading rate and your comprehension score meet. Mark that spot with a dot.
Which quadrant does the dot fall in? Your goal is to be a fluent reader and score in quadrant four.

Review Reading 8: Three Centuries of Hoaxes

THREE CENTURIES OF HOAXES!

A THINKING MACHINE

In 1769, long before computers were invented, a man from Hungary built a wonderful machine that could play chess very well. It delighted people all over Europe and beat nearly
5　everyone it played, including famous figures like French leader Napoleon Bonaparte, and scientist and inventor Benjamin Franklin. For decades, many people believed that it was truly a thinking machine. There were people who said it was a hoax, but could not prove it or explain how it worked. Some 85 years
10　later, the secret was finally revealed. There was a man hiding inside the machine all along...who was obviously very good at playing chess!

ZOO ESCAPE

On November 9, 1874, New York newspaper, *The Herald*, ran a shocking story on its front page. It
15　claimed that all the animals in the Central Park Zoo had escaped and were running around the city. It said the police were working to rescue people, but 27 people had already been killed, and 200 people hurt. It warned everyone to stay at home to avoid danger. Many people in New York were terrified, and did as the paper said. If only they had read the final words of the article, which said: "Not one word of it is true. Not a single act or incident described has taken place." It was all just a hoax. The story
20　was made up by Thomas Connery, an editor at *The Herald*, who wanted to draw attention to the poor condition of cages in the zoo.

ROSIE THE RUNNER

The first woman to cross the finish line of the 1980 Boston Marathon was 23-year-old Rosie Ruiz. However, as she climbed the stairs to receive her prize, people 25 started to become suspicious. She didn't seem to be sweaty or tired. Furthermore, none of the other runners remembered seeing her, and her picture never appeared in photographs or TV broadcasts of the race. Later, several people said that they had seen her join the race 30 only at the end. It turned out she had run only half a mile (about 805 meters) and taken the train for the rest of the race! Her prize was taken away, of course.

---

[1] A **groundskeeper** is the person who takes care of a park or sports ground.

365 words　　**Time taken** _____

Reading Comprehension

Choose the correct answers for the following questions.

1 The passage is mainly about _____ .
   a embarrassing news from the past
   b false stories that fooled many people
   c how the truth about hoaxes is revealed
   d hoaxes in New York City

2 What is true about all the hoaxes in the passage?
   a They frightened people.
   b They delighted people.
   c They made people suspicious.
   d They fooled a lot of people.

3 What was the secret of the thinking machine?
   a It could play chess very well.
   b There was someone hidden inside it.
   c It used a computer to win games.
   d People thought it was a hoax.

4 How many people were really killed by zoo animals in 1874?
   a none
   b 9
   c 27
   d 200

5 Which is NOT mentioned as a reason people became suspicious of Rosie Ruiz?
   a She wasn't out of breath at the finish line.
   b She was not sweaty like the other runners.
   c No one saw her during most of the race.
   d She didn't appear in TV broadcasts of the race.

6 The title of the passage shows us that the writer thinks that hoaxes _____ .
   a are not new
   b are easily avoided
   c are always cruel
   d usually frighten people

Turn to page 176 to record your reading fluency progress. First, find the vertical line that is closest to your reading rate. Next, how many of the six comprehension questions did you answer correctly? Find the point on the graph where your reading rate and your comprehension score meet. Mark that spot with a dot.
Which quadrant does the dot fall in? Your goal is to be a fluent reader and score in quadrant four.

Vocabulary Index

Unit 1
Chapter 1

encourage /ɛnˈkɜrɪdʒ/ *v.* to give someone confidence, for example, by letting them know that what they did is good: *When things aren't going well, he encourages me.*

hands-on /ˈhændzˈɒn/ *adj.* actually doing a particular thing, rather than just talking about it or getting someone else to do it: *Ninety-nine percent of primary pupils now have hands-on experience of computers.*

healthy /ˈhɛlθi/ *adj.* well and not suffering from any illness: *Most of us need to exercise more to be healthy.*

ingredients /ɪnˈgriːdiəntz/ *n.* things that are used to make something, especially all the different foods you use when you are cooking a particular dish: *Mix together all the ingredients.*

kitchen /ˈkɪtʃən/ *n.* a room that is used for cooking and for household jobs such as washing dishes: *She was in the kitchen preparing dinner for the family.*

qualified /ˈkwɒləˌfaɪd/ *adj.* someone who has the skills or experience in order to work in a particular profession: *There are not enough qualified teachers in the country.*

recipe /ˈresəpi/ *n.* a document that describes how to cook something: *He got a recipe for chocolate cake from the cookbook.*

serve /sɜːrv/ *v.* to give someone food and drinks: *Tonight the restaurant is serving a cold tomato soup.*

_____   _____

_____   _____

Chapter 2

add /æd/ *v.* to put something in or on the other thing, to increase, complete, or improve it: *Add the cheese to the pasta sauce.*

bake /beɪk/ *v.* to cook in the oven without any extra liquid or fat: *Bake the cake for 35 to 50 minutes.*

check /tʃek/ *v.* to make sure that something is correct: *He checked that he had his room key.*

cool /kuːl/ *v.* to become lower in temperature: *I waited for the fan to cool the room.*

melt /melt/ *v.* to change to a liquid, usually when heated: *The snow had melted, but the lake was still frozen solid.*

mix /mɪks/ *v.* to stir or shake together, or combine in some other way, so that it becomes a single substance: *It mixes easily with cold or hot water to make a tasty drink.*

pour /pɔːr/ *v.* to make a liquid flow steadily out of a container by holding the container at an angle: *Heat the oil in a frying-pan, then pour in the egg mixture.*

spray /spreɪ/ *v.* to cover or scatter an area: *Remember to spray the flowers with water twice a day.*

_____   _____

_____   _____

Unit 2
Chapter 1

beat /biːt/ *v.* to do better than someone in a competition: *In yesterday's games, Switzerland beat the United States two-one.*

champion /ˈtʃæmpiən/ *n.* someone who has won the first prize in a competition, contest, or fight: *She is a champion boxer and wrestler.*

competitor /kəmˈpetɪtər/ *n.* a person who takes part in a competition or contest: *Herbert Blocker of Germany, one of the oldest competitors, won the silver medal.*

confident /ˈkɒnfɪdənt/ *adj.* to be sure of your ability or idea, or that something is true or : *I am confident that people will believe my story.*

confused /kənˈfyuːzd/ *adj.* not knowing exactly what is happening or what to do: *Things were happening too quickly and Brian was confused.*

machine /məˈʃiːn/ *n.* a piece of equipment which uses electricity or an engine in order to do a particular kind of work: *I put the coin in the machine and pressed the button.*

opponent /əˈpoʊnənt/ *n.* in a contest, your opponent is the person who is playing against you: *Norris knocked down his opponent twice in the early rounds of the fight.*

wonder /ˈwʌndər/ *n.* something that causes people to feel great surprise or admiration: *That building is a wonder.*

_____   _____

_____   _____

Chapter 2

discussion /dɪˈskʌʃən/ *n.* a talk, often in order to reach a decision: *There was a lot of discussion about the report.*

during /ˈdʊərɪŋ/ *prep.* If something happens during a period of time or an event, it happens continuously, or happens several times between the beginning and end of that period or event: *Storms are common during the summer.*

keep in touch /kiːp ɪn tʌtʃ/ *expression v.* to maintain communications with someone or know how they are doing: *I still keep in touch with people I met in university.*

opinion /əˈpɪnyən/ *n.* what you think or believe about something: *I wasn't asking for your opinion.*

surely /ˈʃʊərli/ *adv.* emphasizes that you think something should be true, and you would be surprised if it was not true: *If I can accept this situation, surely you can.*

temperature /ˈtempərətʃər/ *n.* a measure of how hot or cold it is: *The temperature dropped at night.*

useful /ˈyuːsfəl/ *adj.* something that can do something or help you do something: *This book might be useful for people who want to learn how to speak in public.*

vote /voʊt/ *v.* to make your choice officially at a meeting or in an election, for example by raising your hand: *Nearly everyone voted for him at the company meeting.*

_____   _____

_____   _____

Unit 3
Chapter 1

abroad /ə'brɔːd/ *adv.* a foreign country, usually one separated by an ocean or a sea: *I would love to go abroad this year, perhaps to the South of France.*

comfortable /'kʌmftəbəl/ *adj.* to feel confident and relaxed: *She wasn't very comfortable at the party because she didn't know anyone.*

culture /'kʌltʃər/ *n.* the way of life or beliefs of a particular society or civilization: *We must learn to mix with people of different cultures.*

excellent /'eksələnt/ *adj.* very good: *She is excellent at her job.*

exciting /ɪk'saɪtɪŋ/ *adj.* something that makes you feel very happy or enthusiastic: *The race itself is very exciting.*

experience /ɪk'spɪəriəns/ *n.* something that you do or that happens to you, especially something important that affects you: *He had a bad experience with a spider when he was young.*

make sure /meɪk ʃʊər/ *expression v.* check that something is the way you want it to be: *Make sure that you follow the instructions carefully.*

miss /mɪs/ *v.* to feel sad and wish someone you love was with you: *I really miss my sister, who is studying in another country.*

_____ _____

_____ _____

Chapter 2

awesome /'ɔːsəm/ *adj.* someone or something that is very impressive: *The new restaurant has really awesome food.*

embarrassed /em'bærəsd/ *adj.* to feel shy, ashamed, or guilty about something: *He was embarrassed by the tear in his pants.*

hardly /'hɑːrdli/ *adv.* emphasizes that something is very difficult to do: *My garden was covered with so many butterflies that I could hardly see the flowers.*

improve /ɪm'pruːv/ *v.* to get better at something: *He said he was going to improve his football.*

journal /'dʒɜːrnl/ *n.* a record of activities you do every day: *I keep a journal of what I learned in English class.*

lots of /lɒtz əv/ *expression pron.* a large number of something: *We have lots of land to build whatever we want.*

practice /'præktɪs/ *v.* doing something regularly in order to be able to do it better: *I practice speaking English to my parents every day.*

shy /ʃaɪ/ *adj.* nervous and uncomfortable with other people: *She's so shy that she does not speak much to strangers.*

_____ _____

_____ _____

Unit 4
Chapter 1

advice /æd'vaɪs/ *n.* something said to say what you think should be done in a situation: *My advice is to marry your girlfriend.*

average /'ævərɪdʒ/ *n.* a number gotten by adding two more more numbers and then dividing by the total amount of numbers: *The average age of college students is 20.*

borrow /'bɒroʊ/ *v.* to use something that belongs to someone else and that you will give back to them later: *Can I borrow your DVD?*

education /ˌedʒʊ'keɪʃən/ *n.* learning and teaching in a school: *The price of education at a private school is very high.*

list /lɪst/ *v.* to write many things, names, or numbers so you can remember or check them: *In her diary, Jenny lists all the things she needs to do each day.*

per /pɜːr / *prep.* for each: *You need to buy one ticket per person.*

personal /'pɜːrsənl/ *adj.* belonging to one person and not to a group: *Paul has a personal bank account that his wife does not use.*

worry /'wɜːri/ *v.* to be unhappy and think a lot about a person or event: *I am worried about my sister.*

_____   _____

_____   _____

Chapter 2

earn /ɜːrn/ *v.* to get money or other things by working: *How do you earn a living?*

interest /'ɪntərəst, 'ɪntrɪst/ *n.* money that must be paid to the bank when you borrow money: *If you do not pay your credit card, you will owe the bank interest.*

owe /oʊ/ *v.* to need to pay money to someone: *Will paid me $400 but he still owes me $200.*

rent /rent/ *n.* the amount of money paid for the use of a piece of property: *The rent for a one-bedroom apartment is $800 a month.*

second-hand /'sekənd hænd/ *adj.* used by someone else before: *We bought a second-hand car that has 25,000 miles on it.*

split /splɪt/ *v.* to divide among people: *We split a large sandwich.*

stick to /stɪk tu/ *expression v.* to persist, continue: *Is it easy to stick to your budget?*

transportation /ˌtrænspər'teɪʃən/ *n.* ways to move from one place to another: *The fastest method of transportation is by plane, but traveling by bus is cheapest.*

_____   _____

_____   _____

Unit 5
Chapter 1

address /əˈdres/ *v.* to speak about: *She addressed the issue at the meeting.*

annoying /əˈnɔɪ/ *adj.* making you feel slightly angry: *Getting something different than what you ordered is very annoying.*

attention /əˈtenʃən/ *n.* looking and listening: *His attention to his work was interrupted by the telephone.*

combination /ˌkɑːmbəˈneɪʃən/ *n.* two or more things, ideas, or events put together: *Chicken soup is a combination of pieces of chicken, vegetables, and water.*

constantly /ˈkɑːnstənti:/ *adv.* all the time, or very often: *Joe is constantly talking on his cell phone.*

convenient /kənˈviːnyənt/ *adj.* easy and comfortable to do or get to: *Our neighborhood is convenient to the stores and subway.*

emergency /ɪˈmɜːdʒənsi:/ *n.* a bad situation that requires immediate attention: *Call the police; this is an emergency!*

impolite /ˈɪmpɒlaɪt/ *adj.* rude and without good manners: *It is impolite to ask too many personal questions.*

_____   _____

_____   _____

Chapter 2

confirmation /ˌkɑːnfəːˈmeɪʃən/ *n.* a document that says an arrangement or plan is definitely happening: *Hotels send confirmation of your reservation through email.*

combine /kɒmˈbaɪn/ *v.* to join two or more things together to make a single thing: *This recipe combines coconut, chocolate, and cream.*

download /ˈdaʊnˌloʊd/ *v.* to move information from the Internet to a computer: *My computer downloads files very slowly.*

frequent /ˈfriːkwənt/ *adj.* happening often: *In my new job, I make frequent trips to Paris.*

imagine /ɪˈmædʒən/ *v.* to think about something and form a picture in your mind: *The little girl likes to imagine that she is a princess.*

local /ˈloʊkəl/ *n.* someone who lives in the area being talked about: *We got directions to a good restaurant from a local.*

prepare /prɪˈpeəʳ/ *v.* to get ready: *The girls spent the afternoon preparing for tonight's dinner party.*

translate /trænsˈleɪt, ˈtrænzˌleɪt/ *v.* to change into another language: *This book was translated into 20 languages.*

typically /ˈtɪpɪkli:/ *adv.* the way something usually happens: *Children typically have many toys in their bedrooms.*

_____   _____

_____   _____

Unit 6
Chapter 1

honor /ˈɑːnə/ *n.* something that makes you feel very proud: *Winning the Nobel Peace Prize is a great honor.*

kick off /kɪk ɑːf/ *expression v.* to start: *The party kicked off with everyone yelling "Surprise!"*

lighting /ˈlaɪtɪŋ/ *n.* the act of starting something, like a candle, to burn: *Richard is responsible for the lighting of the church candles.*

on foot /ɑːn fʊt/ *expression* to go somewhere by walking: *It will take ten minutes to get to the train station on foot.*

requirement /rɪˈkwaɪəmənt/ *n.* something needed or asked for: *Two years' experience is a requirement for the job.*

select /səˈlekt / *v.* to choose specific people or things: *The woman selected a vegetable dish from the menu.*

symbol /ˈsɪmbəl/ *n.* a picture or shape that represents an organization or an idea: *The boys decided their club's symbol would be a snake.*

take place /teɪk pleɪs/ *expression v.* to happen, occur: *The circus takes place once a year in our town.*

_____   _____

_____   _____

Chapter 2

control /kənˈtroʊl/ *v.* to make something or someone do what you want: *We control a computer using a keyboard and mouse.*

judge /ˈdʒʌdʒ/ *v.* to decide who is the winner: *The swimming event will be judged by three people.*

looks like /lʊks laɪk/ *expression v.* to seem the same: *It looks like it's going to snow.*

manage /ˈmænɪdʒ/ *v.* to take care of a business: *If you start your own company you will spend most of your time managing workers and money.*

object /ˈɑːbdʒɪkt/ *n.* the goal or main idea of a game: *The object of basketball is to throw the ball into the net.*

racer /ˈreɪsə/ *n.* a person who competes in a speed competition: *Do you know which racer crossed the finish line first?*

slide /slaɪd/ *v.* to move something over a smooth surface: *The workers helped to slide the boxes across the floor.*

take a wrong turn /teɪk eɪ rɑːŋ tɜn/ *expression v.* to go in the wrong direction: *You don't want to take a wrong turn and end up on the other side of town.*

_____   _____

_____   _____

Unit 7
Chapter 1

claim /kleɪm/ *v.* to say that something is true even though you are not sure if it is: *He claims to be an expert on the subject.*

despite /dɪˈspaɪt/ *prep.* used to introduce a fact even though something might have prevented it: *She did well on her exams despite not studying.*

establish /ɪˈstæblɪʃ/ *v.* to create or introduce something that will last for a long time: *The school was established in 1989 by an Italian professor.*

forbidden /fərˈbɪdn, fɔrˈbɪdn/ *adj.* not allowed to do or have something: *Drinks are forbidden in the theater.*

former /ˈfɔrmɚ/ *adj.* someone who used to have a particular job, position, or role, but no longer has it: *The former principal of my school came back to give a speech.*

found /faʊnd/ *v.* to get an institution or company started, often by providing the necessary money: *The Independent Labour Party was founded in Bradford on January 13, 1893.*

subject /ˈsʌbdʒɪkt/ *n.* an area of knowledge or study, especially one that you study at school, college, or university: *My favorite subject at school is English.*

survive /səˈvaɪv/ *v.* to continue to exist even after being in a dangerous situation or existing for a long time: *I'm not sure if my house will survive another earthquake.*

_____   _____

_____   _____

Chapter 2

century /ˈsentʃəriː/ *n.* a time period of 100 years: *Many scientific discoveries were made during the 20th century (1901-2000).*

efficient /ɪˈfiʃənt/ *adj.* do tasks successfully, without wasting time or energy: *We must think of a more efficient way to finish this project.*

engineering /endʒəˈnɪːrɪŋ/ *n.* the science and mathematics of making machines, roads, bridges, etc.: *You must study engineering if you want to know how to build a bridge.*

flood /flʌd/ *v.* to cover dry land with water: *The river ran over its banks and flooded the town.*

natural /ˈnætʃərəl/ *adj.* describes things that exist or occur in nature and are not made or caused by people: *The recent typhoon is the worst natural disaster in South Korea in many years.*

prize /praɪz/ *n.* something valuable given to the winner of a competition or game: *First prize in the competition was a new car.*

rotate /ˈroʊˈteɪt/ *v.* to move around something, especially in a circle: *Planets rotate around the sun.*

threaten /ˈθretn/ *v.* to say you will hurt someone: *Tabatha threatened to fire her assistant unless his work improved.*

_____   _____

_____   _____

Unit 8
Chapter 1

calculate /ˈkælkyəˌleɪt/ *v.* to do math: *Can you calculate how much money we will need for the trip?*

develop /dɪˈveləp/ *v.* to happen, occur: *Over the Pacific Ocean, the storm developed from a few rain clouds into a strong typhoon.*

exist /ɪgˈzɪst/ *v.* to be present in the world as a real thing: *He thought that if he couldn't see something, it didn't exist.*

originate /əˈrɪdʒəˌneɪt/ *v.* to begin, come from: *Automobiles originated in the 19th century.*

primary /ˈpraɪˌmeri/ *adj.* something that is very or most important to someone or something: *His difficulty with language was the primary cause of his problems.*

replace /rɪˈpleɪs/ *v.* to take the place of someone or something: *Her boss retired, and she replaced him.*

situation /ˌsɪtʃəˈweɪʃən/ *n.* the way things are at a certain time, what's happening: *The leaders are meeting to talk about the situation in their countries.*

variety /vəˈraɪyəti:/ *n.* different types of things: *That store carries a wide variety of goods, from clothes to furniture.*

_____   _____

_____   _____

Chapter 2

communicate /kəˈmyu:nəˌkeɪt/ *v.* to give information to others: *People communicate by spoken or written language or by body movements.*

demonstrate /ˈdemənˌstreɪt/ *v.* to show people how something works or how to do it: *The trainer will demonstrate how to do an exercise.*

formal /ˈfoɚməl/ *adj.* very or too proper: *He's a difficult person to get to know because he is always so formal.*

get the hang of /get ðə hæŋ əv/ *expression v.* to understand how to do something: *If you practice hard, you will soon get the hang of it.*

introductory /ˌɪntrəˈdʌktəri:/ *n.* a small amount of general information about a particular subject: *My college has introductory classes for people who are interested in learning a new language.*

practical /ˈpræktɪkəl/ *adj.* useful: *A computer would be a practical gift for a student.*

similar /ˈsɪmələɚ/ *adj.* almost alike: *She has a blue dress similar to yours, but hers has a green collar.*

stand for /stænd foɚ/ *expression v.* when a letter or symbol is used to represent a word or an idea: *RSVP stands for a French phrase that asks people invited to an event to please send a reply.*

_____   _____

_____   _____

Unit 9

Chapter 1

celebrate /ˈseləˌbreɪt/ *v.* to do something special (like having a party) for an occasion: *I celebrated my birthday with friends in my favorite restaurant.*

dedicated to /ˈdediˌkeɪtɪd tu:/ *expression v.* give a lot of time and effort to something because they think that it is important: *He's quite dedicated to his students.*

festival /ˈfestəvəl/ *n.* a public celebration, usually for a special reason: *On Norway's independence day, the Norwegians in my town hold a festival with singing and dancing .*

flashy /ˈflæʃi:/ *adj.* showy: *He wears flashy clothes and drives an expensive sports car.*

mask /mæsk/ *n.* something a person wears to cover their face, especially to hide their identity: *In some versions of the story Cinderella wears a mask so no one recognizes her at the dance.*

parade /pəˈreɪd/ *n.* an orderly movement of people in uniforms or colorful costumes, usually to show pride or to honor a special day or event: *On Halloween, people dress in their best costumes and march in a parade down Main Street.*

reunion /riˈyuːnyən/ *n.* a party attended by members of the same family, school, or other group who have not seen each other for a long time: *The society holds an annual reunion.*

spread /spred/ *v.* to gradually reach or affect a larger and larger area or more and more people: *He was angry with the lies being spread about him.*

_____   _____

_____   _____

Chapter 2

ceremony /ˈserəˌmoʊni:/ *n.* a formal event, usually with rituals: *The priest performed a marriage ceremony.*

check in /ˈtʃek ɪn/ *expression v.* to arrive and arrange your stay at a hotel: *I'll call the hotel to let them know we'll check in tomorrow.*

dare /deɚ/ *v.* to do something that requires courage: *Most people hate Harry, but they wouldn't dare to say so.*

display /dɪˈspleɪ/ *v.* to put something in a particular place so that people can see it easily: *All our family photos are displayed in the living room.*

especially /ɪˈspeʃəli:/ *adv.* used to emphasize a characteristic or quality: *The brain is especially sensitive, and even a minute without oxygen can cause problems.*

fascinating /ˈfæsəˌneɪtɪŋ/ *adj.* very interesting and attractive: *Madagascar is the most fascinating place I have ever been to.*

greet /griːt/ *v.* to say hello to someone: *When I met the president, she greeted me in a very friendly way.*

separate /ˈsepərət/ *adj.* several different things, rather than just one thing: *Men and women have separate exercise rooms.*

_____   _____

_____   _____

Unit 10
Chapter 1

allow /əˈlaʊ/ *v.* to let, permit: *We allow our son to drive the family car.*

consider /kənˈsɪdə/ *v.* an opinion of what something or someone is: *I consider Barbara my best friend.*

employ /ɪmˈplɔɪ/ *v.* to pay someone to work for you: *The company employs 18 people.*

no longer /noʊ ˈlɑːŋgə/ expression *adv.* not any more: *Bobby is tired and no longer wants to go to the park.*

prohibit /proʊˈhɪbət/ *v.* to forbid, to ban by order or law: *The law prohibits people from killing each other.*

retirement /rɪˈtayəmənt/ *n.* the period of your life when you stop working completely: *My dad will reach retirement age soon.*

significant /sɪgˈnɪfɪkənt/ *adj.* something that is important or shows something: *On New Year's Day people plan ways to make significant changes to their lives.*

transition /trænˈzɪʃən/ *n.* a change from one condition to another: *The transition from high school to college can be difficult for young people.*

_____   _____

_____   _____

Chapter 2

freedom /ˈfriːdəm/ *n.* having the power to do what you want: *The dog is not in a cage and has the freedom to go wherever he wants to go.*

gradually /ˈgrædʒəwəliː/ *adv.* happening slowly or by small steps: *Gradually, I got used to life in the city.*

independent /ˌɪndəˈpendənt/ *adj.* free, able to do things by yourself and in your own way: *Claire spent her last day in Japan independent of her boyfriend.*

interview /ˈɪntəˌvyuː/ *v.* to ask a person questions to get information: *A TV reporter interviewed the mayor about the city's problems.*

migrate /ˈmaɪˌgreɪt/ *v.* to move to a different country or place: *Birds migrate from cold to warm areas of the world each year.*

overcome /ˌoʊvəˈkʌm/ *v.* to deal with and solve a problem: *Not having much space in a store can be overcome by using tall shelves.*

reluctant /rɪˈlʌktənt/ *adj.* to be unwilling to do something: *I'm a bit reluctant to start riding a scooter; I'd prefer to drive a car.*

suburb /ˈsʌˌbəb/ *n.* a small city or town outside a large city: *There are many cars in the suburbs.*

_____   _____

_____   _____

Unit 11
Chapter 1

adjust /əˈdʒʌst/ *v.* to change something slightly so that it is more effective or appropriate: *The shop must adjust its hours to attract more customers.*

ancient /ˈeɪnʃənt/ *adj.* belonging to the distant past; very old: *The people of ancient Greece helped create modern western culture.*

associate /əˈsouʃiˌeɪt/ *v.* to link or connect with: *Dark clouds are usually associated with thunder storms.*

break up /breɪk ʌp/ *expression v.* separated or divided into several smaller parts: *Break the chocolate bar up into six pieces.*

come up with /kʌm ʌp wɪθ/ *expression v.* to think of a plan or idea and suggest it: *The purpose of today's meeting is to come up with ways to earn money.*

connect /kənekt/ *v.* to put or join together: *The printer cord must be connected to the computer and to a source of electricity for it to work.*

keep track of /kiːp træk ʌv/ *expression v.* to make sure that you have the newest and most accurate information about something all the time: *With 50 students in a class, it's very difficult for a teacher to keep track of everyone.*

switch /swɪtʃ/ *v.* to change to something different: *Sarah's hair was very dry, so she switched to a better shampoo.*

_____   _____

_____   _____

Chapter 2

claim /ˈkleɪm/ *v.* to state that something is true, even though it has not been proved: *Josh claimed he was late because of traffic.*

evidence /ˈevədəns/ *n.* anything seen, experienced, read, or said that shows an event happened: *There is a lot of evidence that stress makes people become sick.*

limit /ˈlɪmət/ *v.* to stop an amount or number from increasing beyond a specific point: *Entry to this contest is limited to people living in Ontario.*

oddly /ˈɑːdliː/ *adv.* strange or unusual: *Why is Greg behaving so oddly today?*

recent /ˈriːsn̩t/ *adj.* in the past but not very long ago, such as yesterday, last week, or last month: *I recently visited my parents.*

sense /ˈsens/ *v.* to become aware of something, although it is not very obvious: *A mother can sense when her child is in pain.*

take into account /teɪk ɪntu əˈkaʊnt/ *expression v.* to allow or plan for something: *We should take into account that there will be vegetarians at the party, so let's prepare some non-meat dishes.*

truth /truːθ/ *n.* the facts about a situation, rather than what is imagined or invented: *The truth is that I broke your television.*

_____   _____

_____   _____

Unit 12
Chapter 1

greedy /ˈgriːdiː/ *adj.* to desire money, food, etc.: *He is a greedy man. No amount of money will ever be enough for him.*

request /rɪˈkwest/ *v.* to ask for something: *The teacher requested the class be quiet.*

luxurious /ˌlʌgˈʒɜːriyəs/ *adj.* very comfortable and expensive: *Roberto enjoyed his luxurious lifestyle.*

delicate /ˈdelɪkət/ *adj.* small and beautifully shaped: *A harp player must have delicate hands.*

delight /dɪˈlaɪt/ *n.* happiness, joy: *Patty jumped up in delight.*

dish /dɪʃ/ *n.* plates, bowls, and platters used to serve and hold food: *Please put more vegetables on your dish.*

declare /dɪˈkleɚ/ *v.* to say that something is true in a firm, deliberate way: *William declared his intention to become the best golfer in the world.*

out of breath /aʊt ʌv breθ/ *expression adj.* to have difficulty breathing: *You should exercise more if you become out of breath after climbing a few stairs.*

_____   _____

_____   _____

Chapter 2

obtain /əbˈteɪn/ *v.* to get or achieve something: *The color purple can be obtained by mixing red and blue.*

fare /feɚ/ *n.* the price for a ride on something, like a taxi or a bus: *If we take a taxi together, we can share the fare.*

promotion /prəˈmoʊʃən/ *n.* advertising to help sell something: *The store had a buy-one-get-one-free promotion.*

terrible /ˈterəbəl/ *adj.* horrible, very bad: *Did you see the terrible car accident on the highway?*

immense /ɪˈmens/ *adj.* very large: *There is an immense statue in the middle of the park.*

fool /fuːl/ *v.* to trick or deceive someone: *On April 1, people try their best to fool their friends.*

shock /ʃɑːk/ *n.* something that is unpleasant, upsetting, or very surprising: *It was a shock to learn Vivian wanted to quit her job.*

hoax /hoʊks/ *n.* something that is not true, a trick: *The bomb threat turned out to be a hoax.*

_____   _____

_____   _____

Prefixes and Suffixes

Here is a list of prefixes and suffixes that appear in this book.

Prefixes

a, ad movement to or change into: *advance*, *arrive*, *attend*; **best-** most: ***best***-*known*, ***best***-*loved*; **bi** two: ***bi***athlon, ***bi***cycle; **com, con** with, together: ***com***municate, ***com***pare, ***con***nect, ***con***tain; **dis** not, negative: ***dis***agree, ***dis***approve; **en** to put in the state or condition of: ***en***courage, ***en***sure; **ex** related to outside or away: ***ex***pense, ***ex***port, ***ex***troverted; **im, in** not, negative: ***im***polite, ***in***dependent, ***in***sensitive, ***in***consistent; **im, in** related to inside, or inwards: ***im***port, ***in***come, ***in***ternal; **inter** between two or more places or groups: ***Inter***net, ***inter***national; **kilo** *a thousand*: ***kilo***meter, ***kilo***watt; **micro** very small: ***micro***phone, ***micro***wave; **mid** referring to the middle: ***mid***dle, ***mid***night; **mis** badly or wrongly: ***mis***take, ***mis***understand; **over** too much: ***over***eat, ***over***weight; **pre** before in time, place, order, or importance: ***pre***vent, ***pre***dict, ***pre***pare; **re** do something again: ***re***use, ***re***appear, ***re***vise; **sub** below, under: ***sub***heading, ***sub***marine, ***sub***merge, ***sub***title, ***sub***way; **tele** far: ***tele***phone, ***tele***vision; **trans** across: ***trans***portation, ***trans***late, ***trans***ition; **un** not, negative: ***un***comfortable, ***un***fortunate, ***un***healthy, ***un***sure; **uni** one: ***uni***ted, ***uni***versity; **up** higher or improved: ***up***hill, ***up***grade, ***up***date; **well-** done well, or a lot: ***well***-*known*, ***well***-*liked*

Suffixes

able full of: *comfort**able***, *knowledge**able***, *valu**able***; **able, ible** able to be: *believ**able***, *enjoy**able***, *vis**ible***; **al** used to make an adjective from a noun: *addition**al***, *nation**al***, *person**al***; **an, ian** relating to (usually, to a country): *Americ**an***, *Austral**ian***, *Canad**ian***, *Ital**ian***; **ant, ent** one who does something: *applic**ant***, *particip**ant***, *stud**ent***; **ant, ent** indicating an adjective: *import**ant***, *independ**ent***; **ary, ery** act or place of doing something: *bak**ery***, *robb**ery***, *mis**ery***; **ate** used to make a verb from a noun: *celebr**ate***, *origin**ate***; **dom** state of being: *free**dom***; **ed** used to form adjectives from verbs: *depress**ed***, *excit**ed***, *interest**ed***; **eer** one who does something: *engin**eer***; **en** used to form verbs meaning to increase a quality: *fright**en***, *hard**en***, *threat**en***; **ence** added to some adjectives to make a noun: *excell**ence***, *prefer**ence***; **ent** used to make an adjective from a verb: *differ**ent***, *excell**ent***; **er, or** someone or something that does something: *air condition**er***, *competit**or***, *comput**er***, *learn**er***, *report**er***, *teach**er***; **er** (after an adjective) more: *saf**er***, *fast**er***; **ese** relating to (usually, to an Asian; country): *Chin**ese***, *Japan**ese***; **est** (after an adjective) most: *clos**est***, *earli**est***, *thinn**est***; **ever** any: *what**ever***; **ful** with, full of: *beauti**ful***, *color**ful***, *forget**ful***, *use**ful***; **hood** state or condition: *adult**hood***, *child**hood***; **ic** used to make an adjective: *realist**ic***, *simplist**ic***; **ion, sion, tion** indicating a noun: *combina**tion***, *competi**tion***, *comprehen**sion***, *discus**sion***, *opin**ion***, *relig**ion***; **ine** indicating a verb: *comb**ine***; **ish** relating to: *Engl**ish***, *fool**ish***, *Ir**ish***; **ist** one who does something: *Buddh**ist***, *terror**ist***, *tour**ist***; **ity** used to make a noun from an adjective: *abil**ity***, *celebr**ity***, *personal**ity***; **ive** indicating an adjective: *expens**ive***, *sensit**ive***, *submiss**ive***; **ize** used to make a verb from an adjective: *organ**ize***, *social**ize***; **less** without, not having: *hope**less***, *rest**less***, *thought**less***; **ly** used to form an adverb from an adjective: *careful**ly***, *frequent**ly***; **mate** companion: *class**mate***, *room**mate***; **ment** used to make a noun from a verb: *announce**ment***, *encourage**ment***, *govern**ment***, *require**ment***, *retire**ment***; **ness** used to make a noun from an adjective: *ill**ness***, *foolish**ness***, *weak**ness***; **ous, ious** relating to: *adventur**ous***, *curi**ous***, *danger**ous***, *delici**ous***; *luxuri**ous***; **ship** indicating a noun: *friend**ship***, *member**ship***; **some** full of: *awe**some***, *hand**some***; **th** indicating an order: *eighteen**th***, *fifteen**th***; **ure** indicating some nouns: *cult**ure***, *temperat**ure***; **y** indicating an adjective: *flash**y***, *greed**y***, *health**y***

Reading Rate Chart

Use this graph to record your progress for each of the eight Review Reading passages. Find the intersection of your reading rate and your comprehension score. Write the number of the review reading on the chart. Your goal is to place in Quadrant 4.

335	**Quadrant 2**				**Quadrant 4**
320					
305					
290					
275					
260					
245					
230					
215					
200					
185					
170					
155					
140					
125					
110					
95					
80					
65					
50	**Quadrant 1**				**Quadrant 3**
	1 (20%)	2 (40%)	3 (60%)	4 (80%)	5 (100%)

Calculating your words-per-minute (wpm). At the end of each passage you see the number of words in the text (i.e. Practice Reading #1 = 175 words). Divide your time into the number of words in the passage to get your wpm. For example, if you read Practice Reading #1 in 45 seconds your wpm equals 233 wpm (175/.75 = 233).

Quadrant 1: You are reading slower than 200 wpm with less than 70% comprehension.
Quadrant 2: You are reading faster than 200 wpm with less than 70% comprehension.
Quadrant 3: You are reading slower than 200 wpm with greater than 70% comprehension.
Quadrant 4: You are reading faster than 200 wpm with greater than 70% comprehension.